Brainstem, including: Medulla Oblongata, Pons, List Of Regions In The Human Brain, Midbrain, Medial Lemniscus, Nucleus Ambiguus, Medial Longitudinal Fasciculus, Lateral Lemniscus, Locus Coeruleus, Fourth Ventricle, Cuneate Nucleus, Superior Colliculus

Hephaestus Books

Contents

Articles

References

Medulla oblongata

Medulla oblongata

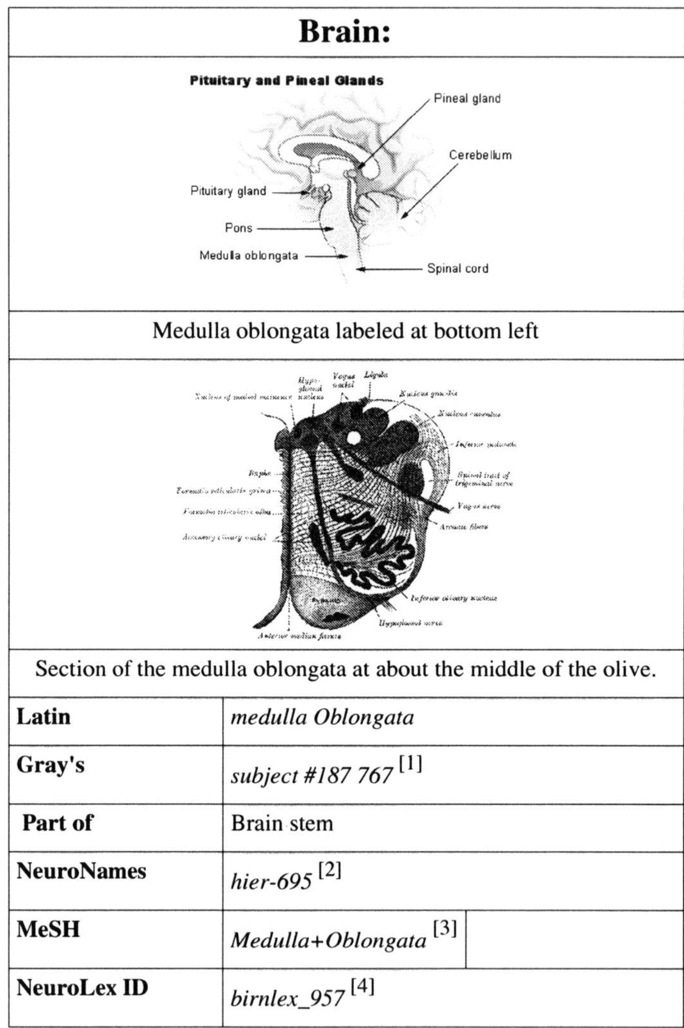

Brain:	
Medulla oblongata labeled at bottom left	
Section of the medulla oblongata at about the middle of the olive.	
Latin	*medulla Oblongata*
Gray's	*subject #187 767* [1]
Part of	Brain stem
NeuroNames	*hier-695* [2]
MeSH	*Medulla+Oblongata* [3]
NeuroLex ID	*birnlex_957* [4]

The **medulla oblongata** is the lower half of the brainstem. In discussions of neurology and similar contexts where no ambiguity will result, it is often referred to as simply **the medulla**. The medulla contains the cardiac, respiratory, vomiting and vasomotor centers and deals with autonomic functions, such as breathing, heart rate and blood pressure.

Anatomy

Two parts: open and closed

The medulla is often thought of as being in two parts:

- an **open part** or superior part where the dorsal surface of the medulla is formed by the fourth ventricle.
- a **closed part** or inferior part where the metacoel lies within the medulla.

Between the anterior median sulcus and the anterolateral sulcus

The region between the anterior median sulcus and the anterolateral sulcus is occupied by an elevation on either side known as the pyramid of medulla oblongata. This elevation is caused by the corticospinal tract.

In the lower part of the medulla some of these fibers cross each other thus obliterating the anterior median fissure. This is known as the decussation of the pyramids.

Some other fibers that originate from the anterior median fissure above the decussation of the pyramids and run laterally across the surface of the pons are known as the external arcuate fibers.

Between the anterolateral and posterolateral sulci

The region between the anterolateral and posterolateral sulc in the upper part of the medulla is marked by a swelling known as the Olivary body.

It is caused by a large mass of gray matter known as the inferior olivary nucleus.

Between the posterior median sulcus and the posterolateral sulcus

The posterior part of the medulla between the posterior median sulcus and the posterolateral sulcus contains tracts that enter it from the posterior funiculus of the spinal cord. These are the fasciculus gracilis, lying medially next to the midline, and the fasciculus cuneatus, lying laterally.

These fasciculi end in rounded elevations known as the gracile and the cuneate tubercles. They are caused by masses of gray matter known as the nucleus gracilis and the nucleus cuneatus.

Just above the tubercles, the posterior aspect of the medulla is occupied by a triangular fossa, which forms the lower part of the floor of the fourth ventricle. The fossa is bounded on either side by the inferior cerebellar peduncle, which connects the medulla to the cerebellum.

Lower part

The lower part of the medulla, immediately lateral to the fasciculus cuneatus, is marked by another longitudinal elevation known as the tuberculum cinereum.

It is caused by an underlying collection of gray matter known as the spinal nucleus of the trigeminal nerve.

The gray matter of this nucleus is covered by a layer of nerve fibers that form the spinal tract of the trigeminal nerve.

Base

The base of the medulla is defined , the commissural fibers, crossing over from the ipsilateral side in the spinal cord to the contralateral side in the brain stem; below this is the spinal.

Functions

The medulla oblongata controls autonomic functions, and relays nerve signals between the brain and spinal cord. It is also responsible for controlling several major points and autonomic functions of the body:

- respiration ----- chemoreceptors
- cardiac center ----- sympathetic, parasympathetic system
- vasomotor center---- baroreceptors
- reflex centers of vomiting, coughing, sneezing, and swallowing
- balancing the human body.

Blood supply

Blood to the medulla is supplied by a number of arteries.

- Anterior spinal artery: The anterior spinal artery supplies the whole medial part of the medulla oblongata. A blockage (such as in a stroke) will injure the pyramidal tract, medial lemniscus, and the hypoglossal nucleus. This causes a syndrome called medial medullary syndrome.
- Posterior inferior cerebellar artery (PICA): The posterior inferior cerebellar artery, a major branch of the vertebral artery, supplies the posterolateral part of the medulla, where the main sensory tracts run and synapse. (As the name implies, it also supplies some of the cerebellum.)
- Direct branches of the vertebral artery: The vertebral artery supplies an area between the other two main arteries, including the nucleus solitarius and other sensory nuclei and fibers. Lateral medullary syndrome can be caused by occlusion of either the PICA or the vertebral arteries.

Additional images

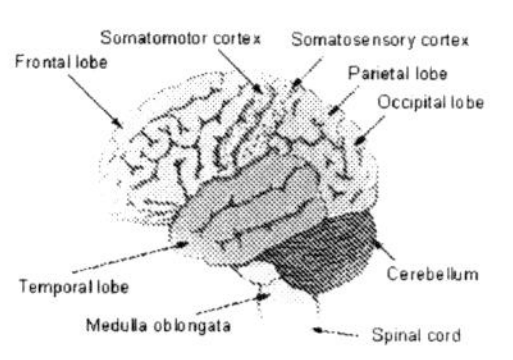

Lobes

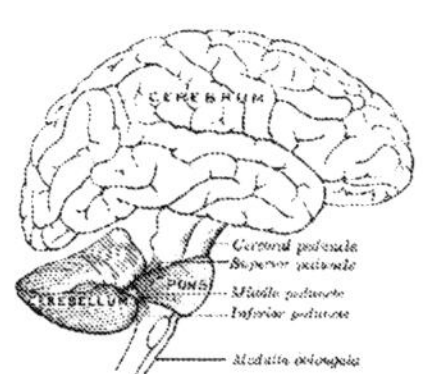

Scheme showing the connections of the several parts of the brain.

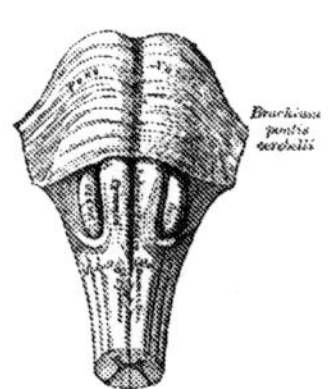

Anteroinferior view of the medulla oblongata and pons.

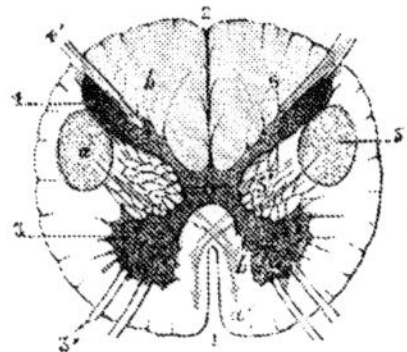

Section of the medulla\ oblongata through the lower part of the decussation of the pyramids

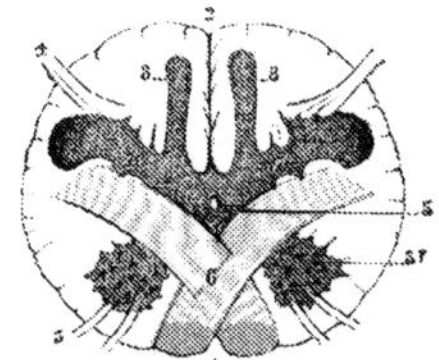

Section of the medulla oblongata at the level of the decussation of the pyramids.

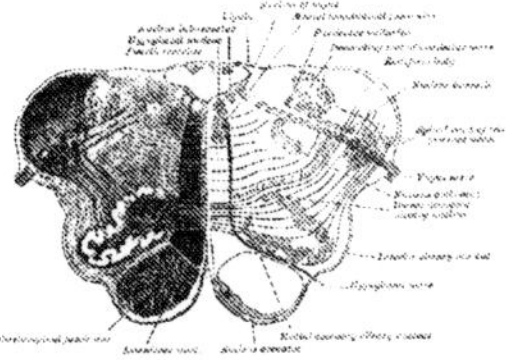

Transverse section of medulla oblongata below the middle of the olive.

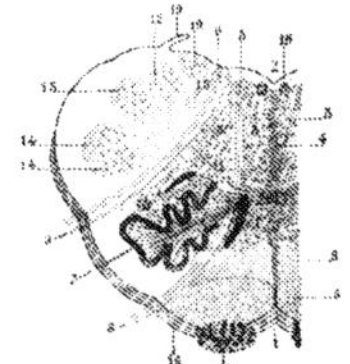

The formatio reticularis of the medulla oblongata, shown by a transverse section passing through the middle of the olive.

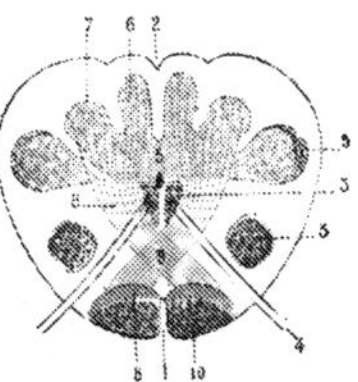

Transverse section passing through the sensory decussation.

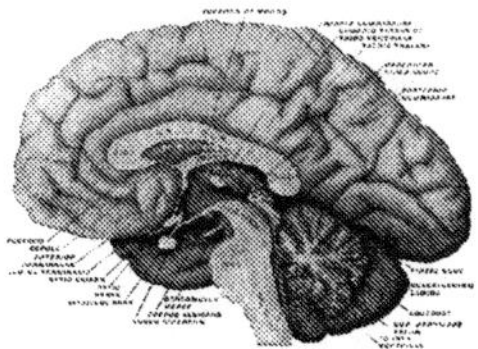

Mesal aspect of a brain sectioned in the median sagittal plane.

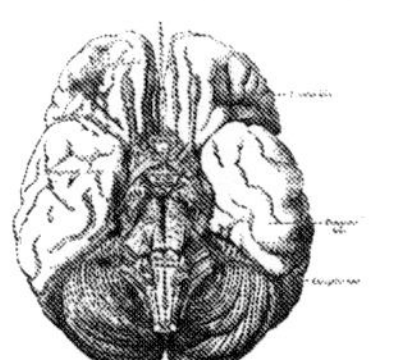

Base of brain.

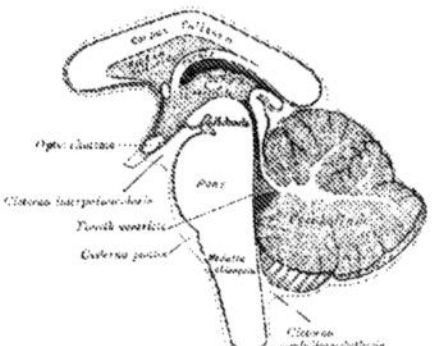

Diagram showing the positions of the three principal subarachnoid cisternæ.

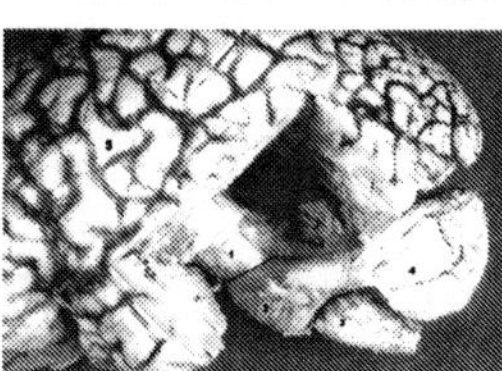

Human cerebrum lateral view

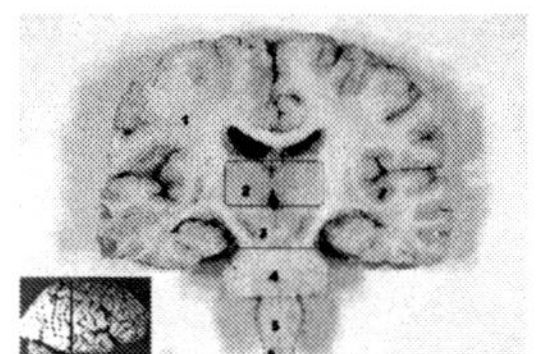

Human brain frontal (coronal) section

External links

- BrainMaps at UCDavis *medulla* [5]

Pons

Pons

Brain: Pons

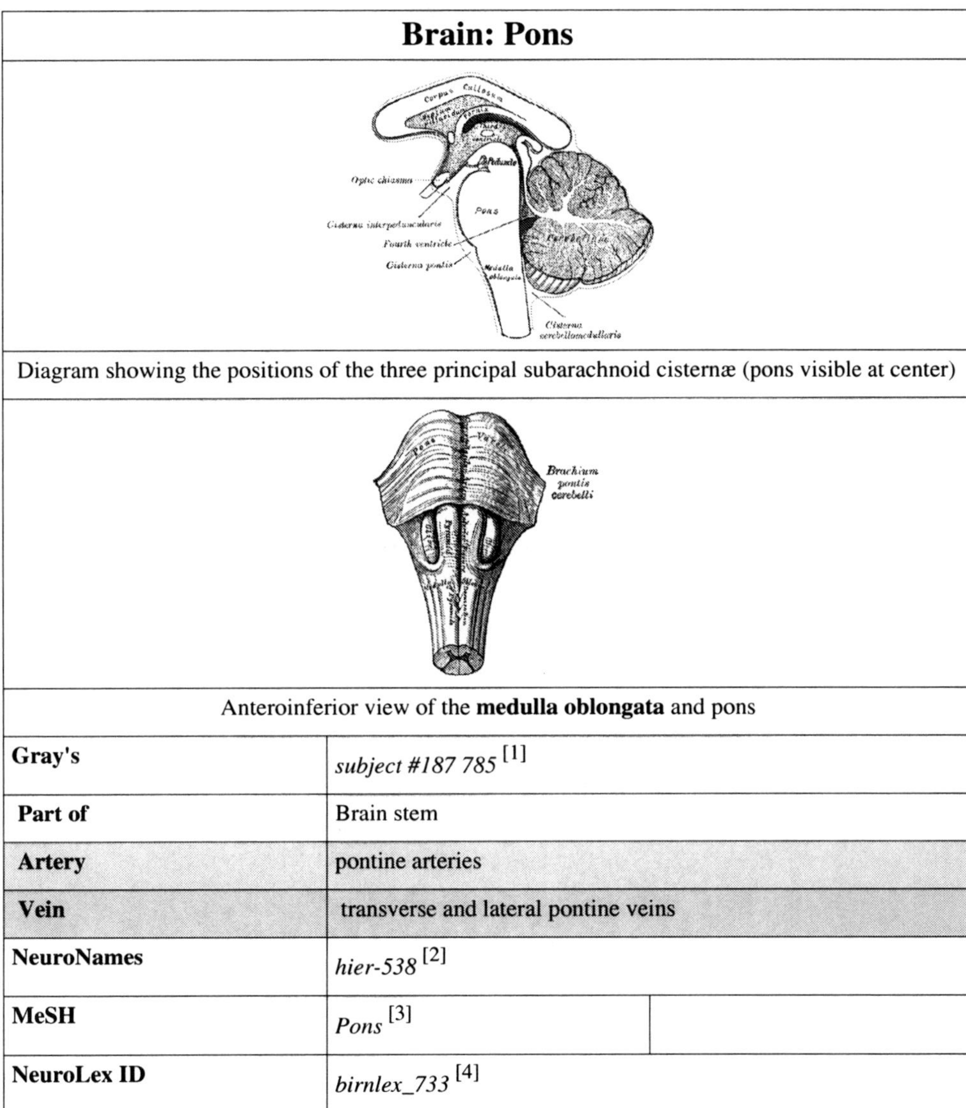

Diagram showing the positions of the three principal subarachnoid cisternæ (pons visible at center)

Anteroinferior view of the **medulla oblongata** and pons

Gray's	*subject #187 785* [1]	
Part of	Brain stem	
Artery	pontine arteries	
Vein	transverse and lateral pontine veins	
NeuroNames	*hier-538* [2]	
MeSH	*Pons* [3]	
NeuroLex ID	*birnlex_733* [4]	

The **pons** (Latin for "bridge"), sometimes **pons Varolii** (after Costanzo Varolio, a 16th-century Italian anatomist and surgeon) is a structure located on the brain stem. It is superior to (up from) the medulla oblongata, inferior to (down from) the midbrain, and ventral to (in front of) the cerebellum. In humans and other bipeds this means it is above the medulla, below the midbrain, and anterior to the cerebellum. This white matter includes tracts that conduct signals from the cerebrum down to the cerebellum and medulla, and tracts that carry the sensory signals up into the thalamus.

The pons measures about 2.5 cm in length. Most of it appears as a broad anterior bulge rostral to the medulla. Posteriorly, it consists mainly of two pairs of thick stalks called cerebellar peduncles. They connect the cerebellum to the pons and midbrain.

The pons contains nuclei that relay signals from the cerebrum to the cerebellum, along with nuclei that deal primarily with sleep, respiration, swallowing, bladder control, hearing, equilibrium, taste, eye movement, facial expressions, facial sensation, and posture.

Within the pons is the pneumotaxic center, a nucleus in the pons that regulates the change from inspiration to expiration.

Embryonic development

During embryonic development the embryonic metencephalon develops into two structures: the pons and the cerebellum.

Cranial nerve nuclei

A number of cranial nerve nuclei are present in the pons:

- mid-pons: The *chief* or *pontine* nucleus of the trigeminal nerve sensory nucleus (V)
- mid-pons: the motor nucleus for the trigeminal nerve (V)
- lower down in the pons: abducens nucleus (VI)
- lower down in the pons: facial nerve nucleus (VII)
- lower down in the pons: vestibulocochlear nuclei (vestibular nuclei and cochlear nuclei) (VIII)

The functions of these four nerves include sensory roles in hearing, equilibrium, and taste, and in facial sensations such as touch and pain; as well as motor roles in eye movement, facial expressions, chewing, swallowing, urination, and the secretion of saliva and tears.

Related diseases

- Central pontine myelinosis, a demyelination disease that causes difficulty with sense of balance, walking, sense of touch, swallowing and speaking. In a clinical setting it is often associated with transplant. Undiagnosed it can lead to death or locked-in syndrome.

Additional images

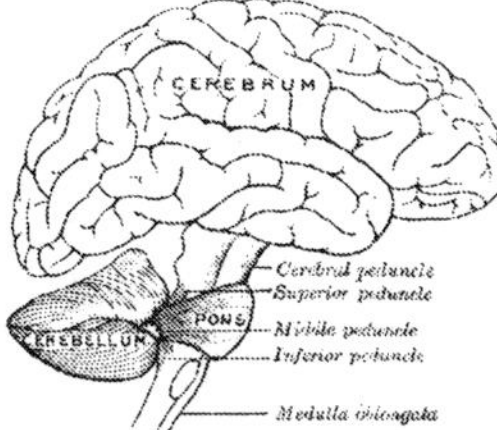

Scheme showing the connections of the several parts of the brain.

Superficial dissection of brain-stem. Lateral view.

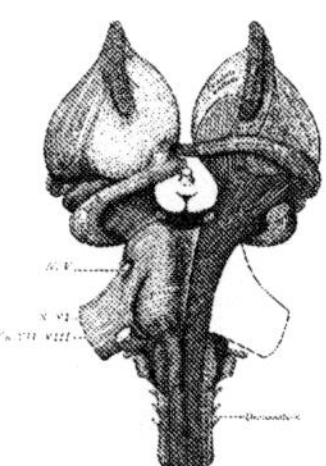

Superficial dissection of brain-stem. Ventral view.

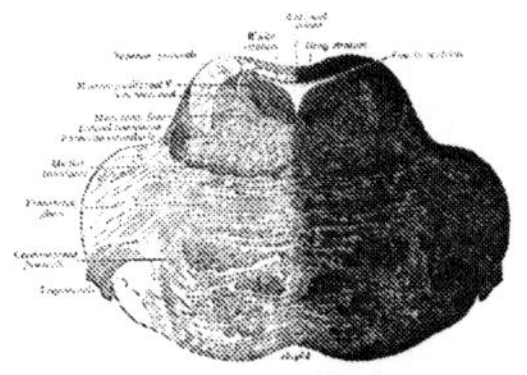

Axial section of the pons, at its upper part.

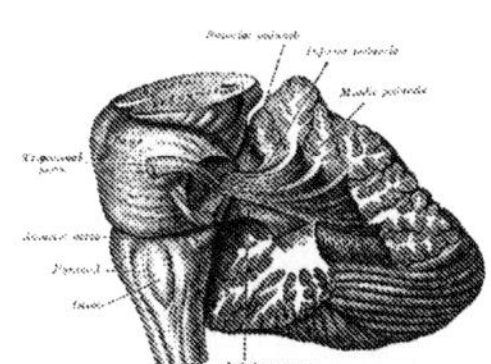

Dissection showing the projection fibers of the cerebellum.

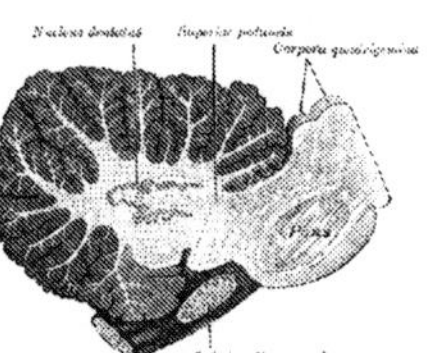

Sagittal section through right cerebellar hemisphere. The right olive has also been cut sagitally.

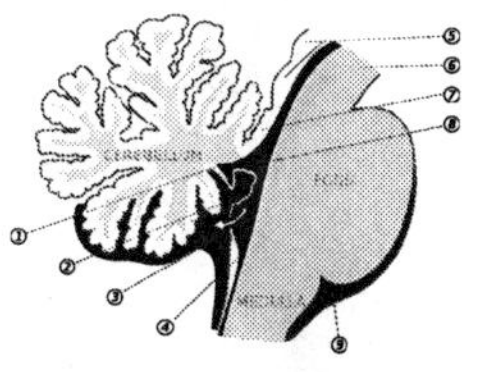

Scheme of roof of fourth ventricle. The arrow is in the foramen of Majendie.

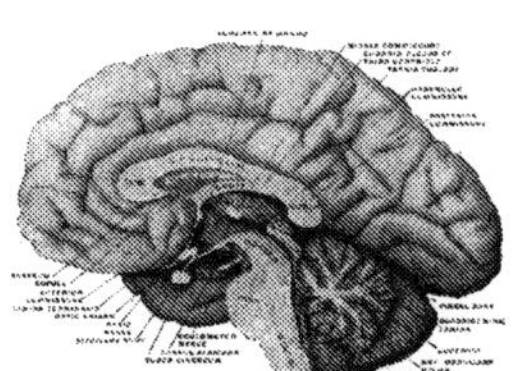

Mesal aspect of a brain sectioned in the median sagittal plane.

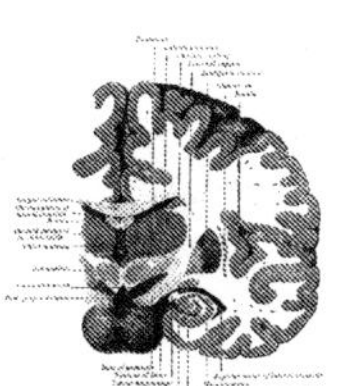

Coronal section of brain immediately in front of pons.

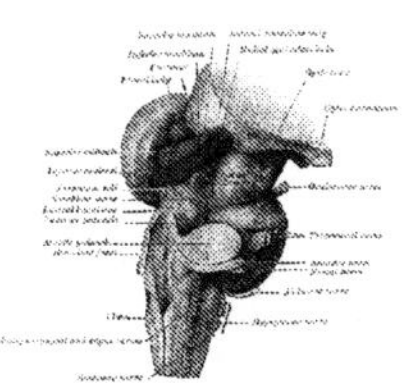

Hind- and mid-brains; postero-lateral view.

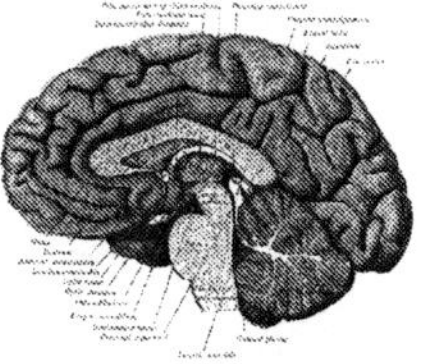

Median sagittal section of brain.

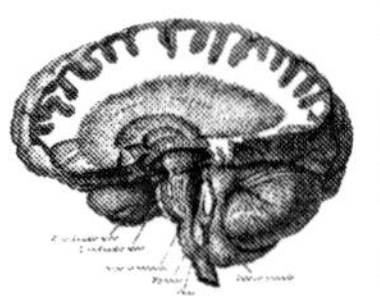

Dissection showing the course of the cerebrospinal fibers.

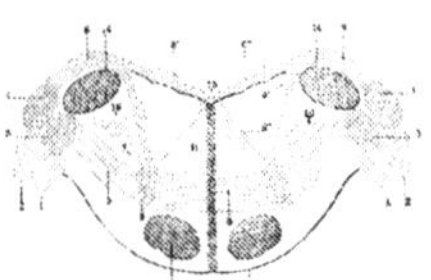

Terminal nuclei of the cochlear nerve, with their upper connections.

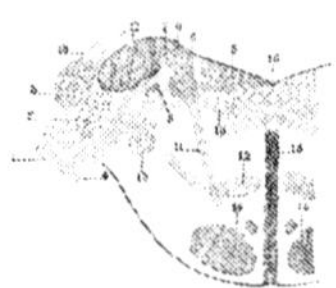

Terminal nuclei of the vestibular nerve, with their upper connections.

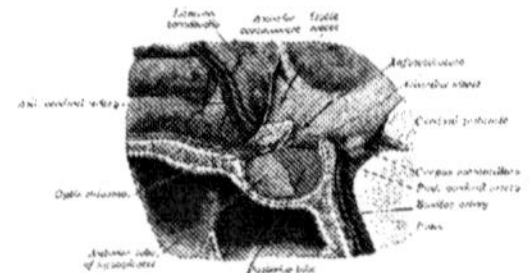

The hypophysis cerebri in position. Shown in sagittal section.

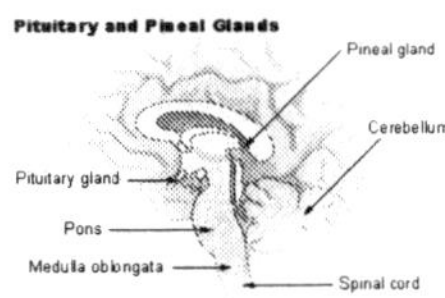

Pituitary and pineal glands

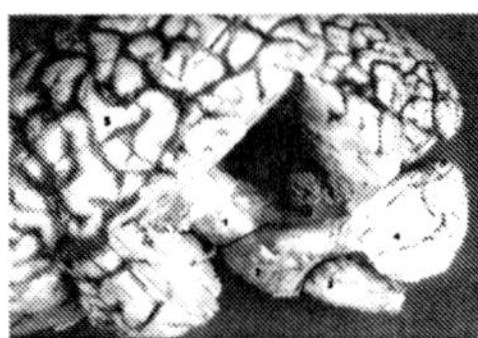

Human cerebrum lateral view

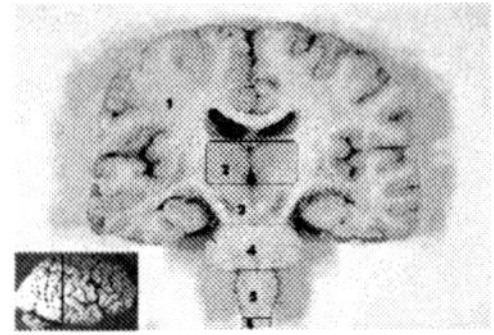

Human brain frontal (coronal) section

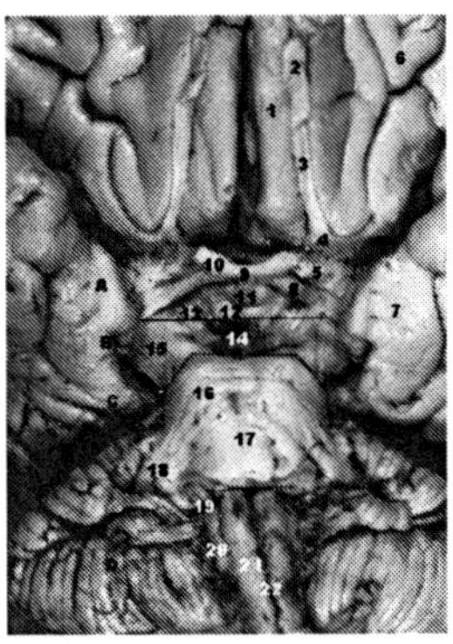

Human brainstem anterior view

References

Saladin Kenneth S.(2007) Anatomy & physiology the unity of form and function. Dubuque, IA: McGraw-Hill

External links

- Diagram at UCC [1]
- BrainMaps at UCDavis *Pons* [2]

Brainstem

Brainstem

Brain: Brainstem	
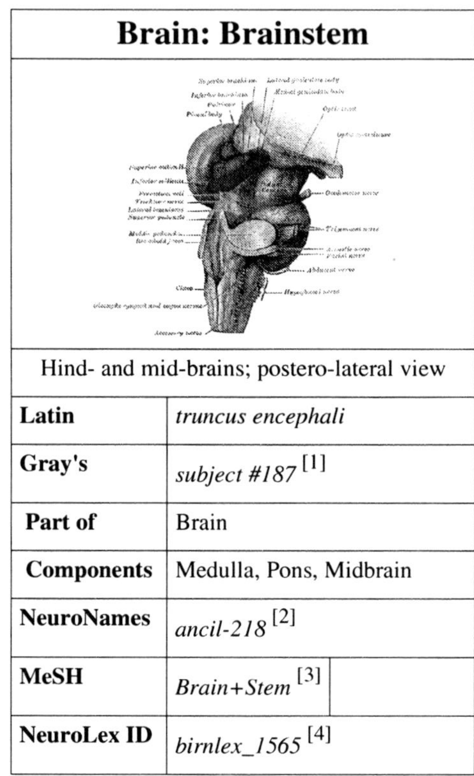	
Hind- and mid-brains; postero-lateral view	
Latin	*truncus encephali*
Gray's	*subject #187* [1]
Part of	Brain
Components	Medulla, Pons, Midbrain
NeuroNames	*ancil-218* [2]
MeSH	*Brain+Stem* [3]
NeuroLex ID	*birnlex_1565* [4]

In vertebrate anatomy the **brainstem** (or **brain stem**) is the posterior part of the brain, adjoining and structurally continuous with the spinal cord. The brain stem provides the main motor and sensory innervation to the face and neck via the cranial nerves. Though small, this is an extremely important part of the brain as the nerve connections of the motor and sensory systems from the main part of the brain to the rest of the body pass through the brain stem. This includes the corticospinal tract (motor), the posterior column-medial lemniscus pathway (fine touch, vibration sensation and proprioception) and the spinothalamic tract (pain, temperature, itch and crude touch). The brain stem also plays an important role in the regulation of cardiac and respiratory function. It also regulates the central nervous system, and is pivotal in maintaining consciousness and regulating the sleep cycle.

It is usually described as including the medulla oblongata (myelencephalon), pons (part of metencephalon), and midbrain (mesencephalon). Less frequently, parts of the diencephalon are included.

General anatomy

Ventral view/medulla and pons

The medial part of the medulla is the anterior median fissure. Moving laterally on each side are the pyramids. The pyramids contain the fibers of the corticospinal tract (also called the pyramidal tract), or the upper motor neuronal axons as they head inferiorly to synapse on lower motor neuronal cell bodies within the ventral horn of the spinal cord.

The anterolateral sulcus is lateral to the pyramids. Emerging from the anterolateral sulci are the hypoglossal nerve (CN XII) rootlets. Lateral to these rootlets and the anterolateral sulci are the olives. The olives are swellings in the medulla containing underlying inferior olivary nuclei (containing various nuclei and afferent fibers). Lateral (and dorsal) to the olives are the rootlets for cranial nerves IX and X (glossopharyngeal and vagus, respectively). The pyramids end at the pontomedullary junction, noted most obviously by the large basal pons. Between the basal pons, cranial nerve 6, 7 and 8 emerge (medial to lateral). These cranial nerves are the abducens nerve, facial nerve and the vestibulocochlear nerve, respectively. At the level of the midpons, the large trigeminal nerve, CN V, emerges. At the rostral pons, the occulomotor nerve emerges at the midline. Laterally, the trochlear nerve has emerged after emerging out of the dorsal rostral pons and wrapping around to the anterior.

Dorsal view/medulla and pons

The most medial part of the medulla is the posterior median fissure. Moving laterally on each side is the fasciculus gracilis, and lateral to that is the fasciculus cuneatus. Superior to each of these, and directly inferior to the obex, are the gracile and cuneate tubercles, respectively. Underlying these are their respective nuclei. The obex marks the end of the 4th ventricle and the beginning of the central canal. The posterior intermediate sulci separates the fasciculi gracilis from the fasciculi cuneatus. Lateral to the fasciculi cuneatus is the lateral funiculus.

Superior to the obex is the floor of the 4th ventricle. In the floor of the 4th ventricle, various nuclei can be visualized by the small bumps that they make in the overlying tissue. In the midline and directly superior to the obex is the vagal trigone and superior to that it the hypoglossal trigone. Underlying each of these are motor nuclei for the respective cranial nerves. Superior to these trigones are fibers running laterally in both directions. These fibers are known collectively as the striae medullares. Continuing in a rostral direction, the large bumps are called the facial colliculi. Each facial colliculus, contrary to their names, do not contain the facial nerve nuclei. Instead, they have facial nerve axons traversing superficial to underlying abducens (CN VI) nuclei. Lateral to all these bumps previously discussed is an indented line, or sulcus that runs rostrally, and is known as the sulcus limitans. This separates the medial motor neurons from the lateral sensory neurons. Lateral to the sulcus limitans is the area collectively known as the vestibular area, which is involved in special sensation. Moving rostrally, the inferior, middle, and superior cerebellar peduncles are found connecting the midbrain to the cerebellum. Directly rostral to the superior cerebellar peduncle, there is the superior medullary velum and then the two trochlear nerves. This marks the end of the pons as the inferior colliculus is directly rostral and marks the caudal midbrain.

Spinal Cord to Medulla Transitional Landmark: From a ventral view, there can be seen a decussation of fibers between the two pyramids. This decussation marks the transition from medulla to spinal cord. Superior to the decussation is the medulla and inferior to it is the spinal cord.

Midbrain

Main article: Midbrain

The midbrain is divided into three parts. The first is the tectum, which is "roof" in Latin. The tectum includes the superior and inferior colliculi and is the dorsal covering of the cerebral aqueduct. The inferior colliculus, involved in the sense of hearing sends its inferior brachium to the medial geniculate body of the diencephalon. Superior to the inferior colliculus, the superior colliculus marks the rostral midbrain. It is involved in the special sense of vision and sends its superior brachium to the lateral geniculate body of the diencephalon. The second part is the tegmentum and is ventral to the cerebral aqueduct. Several nuclei, tracts and the reticular formation are contained here. Last, the ventral side is composed of paired cerebral peduncles. These transmit axons of upper motor neurons.

Midbrain internal structures

Periaqueductal gray: The area around the cerebral aqueduct, which contains various neurons involved in the pain desensitization pathway. Neurons synapse here and, when stimulated, cause activation of neurons in the nucleus raphe magnus, which then project down into the dorsal horn of the spinal cord and prevent pain sensation transmission.

Occulomotor nerve nucleus: This is the nucleus of CN III.

Trochlear nerve nucleus: This is the nucleus of CN IV.

Red Nucleus: This is a motor nucleus that sends a descending tract to the lower motor neurons.

Substantia nigra: This is a concentration of neurons in the ventral portion of the midbrain that uses dopamine as its neurotransmitter and is involved in both motor function and emotion. Its dysfunction is implicated in Parkinson's Disease.

Reticular formation: This is a large area in the midbrain that is involved in various important functions of the midbrain. In particular, it contains lower motor neurons, is involved in the pain desensitization pathway, is involved in the arousal and consciousness systems, and contains the locus ceruleus, which is involved in intensive alertness modulation and in autonomic reflexes.

Central tegmental tract: Directly anterior to the floor of the 4th ventricle, this is a pathway by which many tracts project up to the cortex and down to the spinal cord.

Embryology

The adult human brain stem emerges from two of the three primary vesicles formed of the neural tube. The mesencephalon is the second of the three primary vesicles, and does not further differentiate into a secondary vesicle. This will become the midbrain. The third primary vesicle, the rhombencephalon, will further differentiate into two secondary vesicles, the metencephalon and the myelencephalon. The metencephalon will become the cerebellum and the pons. The myelencephalon will become the medulla.

Functions

There are three main functions of the brain stem:

1. The first is its role in conduction. That is, all information relayed from the body to the cerebrum and cerebellum and vice versa, must traverse the brain stem. The ascending pathways coming from the body to the brain are the sensory pathways, and include the spinothalamic tract for pain and temperature sensation and the dorsal column, fasciculus gracilis, and cuneatus for touch, proprioception, and pressure sensation (both of the body). (The facial sensations have simiar pathways, and will travel in the spinothalamic tract and the medial lemniscus also). Descending tracts are upper motor neurons destined to synapse on lower motor neurons in the ventral horn and intermediate horn of the spinal cord. In addition, there are upper motor neurons that originate in the brain stem's vestibular, red, tectal, and reticular nuclei, which also descend and synapse in the spinal cord.

2. The cranial nerves 3-12 emerge from the brain stem.

3. The brain stem has integrative functions (it is involved in cardiovascular system control, respiratory control, pain sensitivity control, alertness, awareness, and consciousness). Thus, brain stem damage is a very serious and often life-threatening problem.

Physical signs of brain stem disease

Diseases of the brain stem can result to abnormalities in the function of cranial nerves which may lead to visual disturbances, pupil abnormalities, changes in sensation, muscle weakness, hearing problems, vertigo, swallowing and speech difficulty, voice change, and co-ordination problems. Localizing neurological lesions in the brain stem may be very precise, although it relies on a clear understanding on the functions of brain stem anatomical structures and how to test them.

Additional images

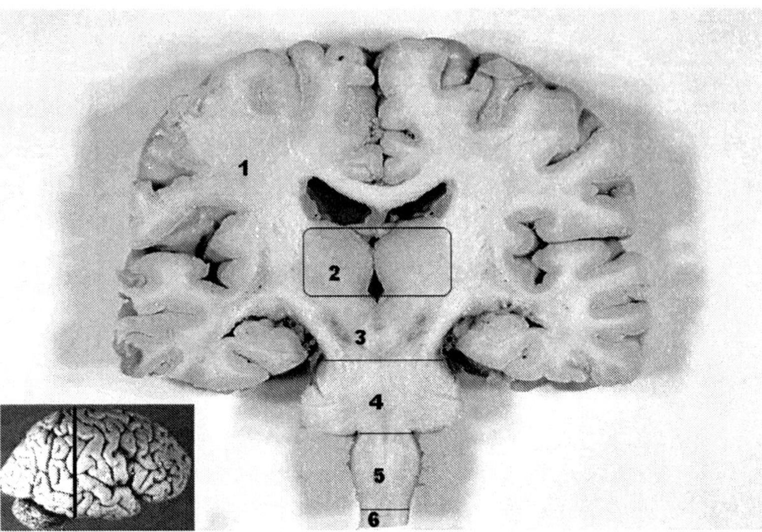

The midbrain, pons, and medulla oblongata are labelled on this coronal section of the human brain.

See also

- Brain stem tumor
- Cranial nerve nucleus
- Reptilian brain
- Comparative Neuroscience at Wikiversity

External links

- http://www.cancerhelp.org.uk/help/default.asp?page=5019
- http://www.meddean.luc.edu/lumen/Meded/Neuro/frames/nlBSsL/nl40fr.htm
- http://biology.about.com/library/organs/brain/blbrainstem.htm
- http://www.waiting.com/brainanatomy.html
- http://www.martindalecenter.com/MedicalAnatomy_3_SAD.html
- NIF Search - Brainstem [5] via the Neuroscience Information Framework

List of regions in the human brain

List of regions in the human brain

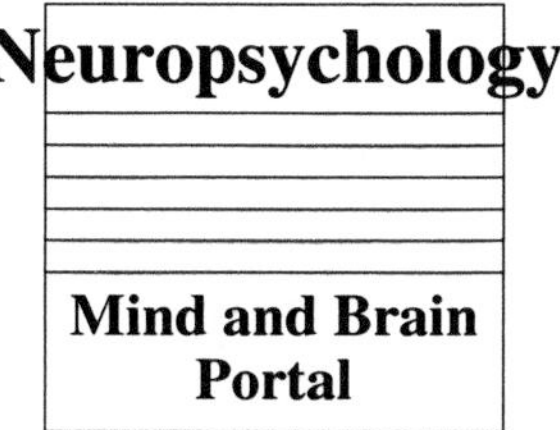

Anatomical regions of the brain are listed vertically, following hierarchies that are standard in neuroanatomy. Functional, connective, and developmental regions are listed horizontally in parentheses where appropriate.

Hindbrain (Rhombencephalon)

Myelencephalon

- medulla oblongata
  - medullary pyramids
  - Medullary cranial nerve nuclei
    - Inferior salivatory nucleus
    - Nucleus ambiguus
    - Dorsal nucleus of vagus nerve
    - Hypoglossal nucleus
    - Solitary nucleus

Metencephalon

- pons
  - Respiratory centres
    - pneumotactic centre
    - apneustic centre
  - Pontine cranial nerve nuclei
    - *chief* or *pontine* nucleus of the trigeminal nerve sensory nucleus (V)
    - motor nucleus for the trigeminal nerve (V)
    - abducens nucleus (VI)
    - facial nerve nucleus (VII)
    - vestibulocochlear nuclei (vestibular nuclei and cochlear nuclei) (VIII)
    - Superior salivatory nucleus
- paramedian pontine reticular formation
- cerebellum
  - cerebellar vermis
  - cerebellar hemispheres
    - anterior lobe
    - posterior lobe
    - flocculonodular lobe
  - cerebellar nuclei
    - fastigial nucleus
    - globose nucleus
    - emboliform nucleus
    - dentate nucleus

Midbrain (mesencephalon)

- tectum
  - inferior colliculi
  - superior colliculi
- mesencephalic duct (cerebral aqueduct, Aqueduct of Sylvius)
- cerebral peduncle
- midbrain tegmentum
  - ventral tegmental area
  - Red Nucleus
  - crus cerebri

- pretectum

Forebrain (prosencephalon)

Diencephalon

Epithalamus

- pineal body
- habenular nuclei
- stria medullares
- tenia thalami

Thalamus

- anterior nuclear group
    - anteroventral nucleus
    - anterodorsal nucleus
    - anteromedial nucleus
- medial nuclear group
    - medial dorsal nucleus
    - midline nuclear group
    - paratenial nucleus
    - reuniens nucleus
    - rhomboidal nucleus
    - intralaminar nuclear group
    - centromedial nucleus
    - parafascicular nucleus
    - paracentral nucleus
    - central lateral nucleus
    - central medial nucleus
- lateral nuclear group
    - lateral dorsal nucleus
    - lateral posterior nucleus
    - pulvinar
- ventral nuclear group
    - ventral anterior nucleus
    - ventral lateral nucleus
    - ventral posterior nucleus

-
  -
    - Ventral posterior lateral nucleus
    - Ventral posterior medial nucleus
- metathalamus
  - medial geniculate body
  - lateral geniculate body
- thalamic reticular nucleus

Hypothalamus ***(limbic system) (HPA axis)***

- Anterior
  - Medial area
    - Parts of preoptic area
      - Medial preoptic nucleus
    - Suprachiasmatic nucleus
    - Paraventricular nucleus
    - Supraoptic nucleus (mainly)
    - Anterior hypothalamic nucleus
  - Lateral area
    - Parts of preoptic area
      - Lateral preoptic nucleus
    - Anterior part of Lateral nucleus
    - Part of supraoptic nucleus
  - Other nuclei of preoptic area
    - median preoptic nucleus
    - periventricular preoptic nucleus
- Tuberal
  - Medial area
    - Dorsomedial hypothalamic nucleus
    - Ventromedial nucleus
    - Arcuate nucleus
  - Lateral area
    - Tuberal part of Lateral nucleus
    - Lateral tuberal nuclei
- Posterior
  - Medial area
    - Mammillary nuclei (part of mammillary bodies)
    - Posterior nucleus

- Lateral area
  - Posterior part of Lateral nucleus
- optic chiasm
- subfornical organ
- periventricular nucleus
- infundibulum
- tuber cinereum
  - tuberal nucleus
  - tuberomamillary nucleus
- tuberal region
- mammillary bodies
- mammillary nucleus

Subthalamus*(HPA axis)*

- thalamic nucleus
- zona incerta

Pituitary gland *(HPA axis)*

- neurohypophysis
- intermediate pituitary
- adenohypophysis

Telencephalon *(cerebrum)* Cerebral hemispheres

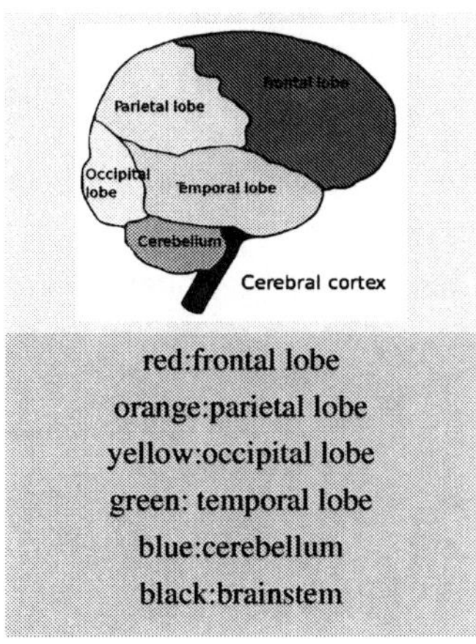

White matter

- Corona radiata
- Internal capsule
- External capsule
- Extreme capsule
- Arcuate fasciculus
- Uncinate fasciculus

Subcortical

- Hippocampus (Medial Temporal Lobe)
- Amygdala *(limbic system) (limbic lobe) (paleopallium)*
  - Central nucleus *(autonomic nervous system)*
  - Medial nucleus *(accessory olfactory system)*
  - Cortical and basomedial nuclei *(main olfactory system)*
  - Lateral and basolateral nuclei *(frontotemporal cortical system)*
- base head *(limbic system) (limbic lobe) (archipallium)*
  - Dentate gyrus
  - *Cornu ammonis* (CA fields)
- Claustrum
- Basal ganglia
  - Striatum*(archipallium)*
    - Dorsal striatum
      - Putamen
      - Caudate nucleus
    - Ventral striatum
      - Nucleus accumbens
      - Olfactory tubercle
  - Globus pallidus (forms nucleus lentiformis with putamen)
  - Subthalamic nucleus
  - Substantia nigra

Rhinencephalon *(paleopallium)*

- Olfactory bulb
- Piriform cortex
- Anterior olfactory nucleus
- Olfactory tract
- Anterior commissure

Cerebral cortex *(neopallium)*

- Frontal lobe
  - Cortex
    - Primary motor cortex (Precentral gyrus, M1)
  - Brodmann area 4 *(Primary motor cortex)*
    - Prefrontal cortex
    - Supplementary motor cortex
    - Premotor cortex
  - Gyrus
    - Superior frontal gyrus
    - Middle frontal gyrus
    - Inferior frontal gyrus
  - Brodmann areas: 6, 8, 9, 10, 11, 12, 24, 25, 32, 33, 44, 45, 46, 47
- Parietal lobe
  - Cortex
    - Primary somatosensory cortex (S1)
    - S2
    - Posterior parietal cortex
  - Gyrus
    - Postcentral gyrus *(Primary somesthetic area)*
  - Other
    - Precuneus
  - Brodmann areas 1, 2, 3 *(Primary somesthetic area)*; 5, 7, 23, 26, 29, 31, 39, 40
- Occipital lobe
  - Cortex
    - Primary visual cortex (V1)
    - V2
  - Gyrus
    - Lateral occipital gyrus

    - Other
        - Cuneus
    - Brodmann areas 17 *(V1, primary visual cortex); 18, 19*
- Temporal lobe
    - Cortex
        - Primary auditory cortex (A1)
        - A2
        - Inferior temporal cortex
        - Posterior inferior temporal cortex
    - Gyrus
        - Superior temporal gyrus
        - Middle temporal gyrus
        - Inferior temporal gyrus
        - Fusiform gyrus
        - Parahippocampal gyrus
    - Brodmann areas: 9, 20, 21, 22, 27, 34, 35, 36, 37, 38, 41, 42
- Insular cortex
- Cingulate cortex
    - Subgenual area 25
    - Anterior cingulate
    - Posterior cingulate
    - Retrosplenial cortex
    - Indusium griseum
    - Brodmann areas 23, 24; 26, 29, 30 *(retrosplenial areas)*; 31, 32

Neural pathways

- arcuate fasciculus
- cerebral peduncle
- corpus callosum
- pyramidal or corticospinal tract
- Major dopamine pathways *dopamine system*
    - mesocortical pathway
    - mesolimbic pathway
    - nigrostriatal pathway
    - tuberoinfundibular pathway
- Serotonin Pathways *serotonin system*

    - Raphe Nuclei

Motor systems

- motor system
    - extrapyramidal system
    - pyramidal tract
    - alpha system
    - gamma system

Nerves

- Spinal cord
- brain stem
    - cranial nerves
        - Cranial nerve, (0)
        - Olfactory nerve, (I)
        - Optic nerve (II)
        - Oculomotor nerve (III)
        - Trochlear nerve(IV)
        - Trigeminal nerve (V)
        - Abducens nerve (VI)
        - Facial nerve (VII)
        - Vestibulocochlear nerve (VIII)
        - Glossopharyngeal nerve (IX)
        - Vagus nerve (X)
        - Accessory nerve (XI)
        - Hypoglossal nerve (XII)

Neuroendocrine systems

- HPA axis

Vascular systems

- venous systems
- circle of Willis (arterial system)
- blood-brain barrier
- blood-cerebrospinal fluid barrier

Dural meningeal system

- brain-cerebrospinal fluid barrier
- meningeal coverings
  - dura mater
  - arachnoid mater
  - pia mater
- epidural space
- subdural space
- arachnoid septum
- ventricular system
  - cerebrospinal fluid
    - subarachnoid space
      - third ventricle
      - fourth ventricle
      - lateral ventricles
        - Anterior horn
        - Body of lateral ventricle
        - Inferior horn
        - Posterior horn
      - superior cistern
      - cistern of lamina terminalis
      - chiasmatic cistern
      - interpeduncular cistern
      - pontine cistern
      - cisterna magna
    - spinal subarachnoid space

Related topic

- Human brain

External links

- High-Resolution Cytoarchitectural Primate Brain Atlases [1]
- View information on various brain regions: images, name in seven languages, location, etc. [2]

Midbrain

Midbrain

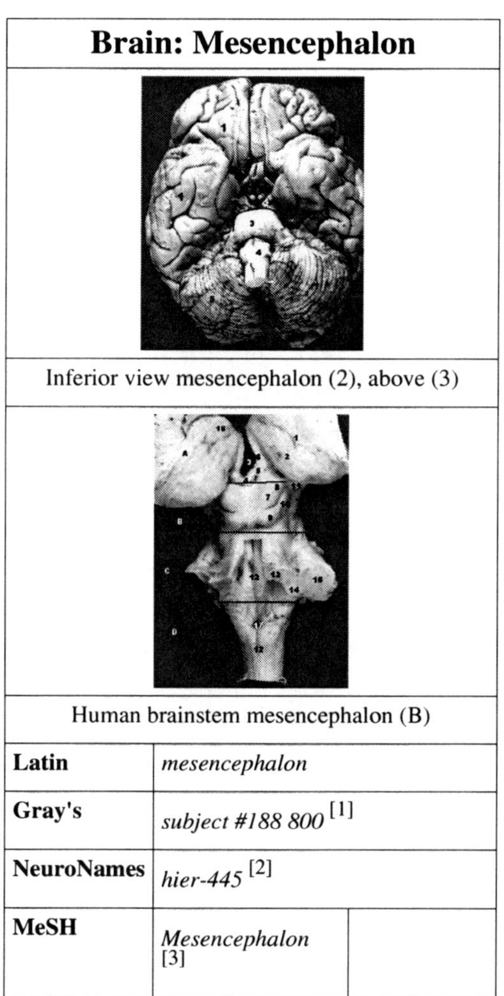

Brain: Mesencephalon	
Inferior view mesencephalon (2), above (3)	
Human brainstem mesencephalon (B)	
Latin	*mesencephalon*
Gray's	*subject #188 800* [1]
NeuroNames	*hier-445* [2]
MeSH	*Mesencephalon* [3]

In biological anatomy, the **mesencephalon** (or **midbrain**) comprises the tectum (or corpora quadrigemina), tegmentum, the ventricular mesocoelia (or "iter"), and the cerebral peduncles, as well as several nuclei and fasciculi. Caudally the mesencephalon adjoins the pons (metencephalon) and rostrally it adjoins the diencephalon (Thalamus, hypothalamus, et al.).

During development, the mesencephalon forms from the middle of three vesicles that arise from the neural tube to generate the brain. In mature human brains, the mesencephalon becomes the least differentiated, from both its developmental form and within its own structure, among the three vesicles. The mesencephalon is considered part of the brain stem. Its substantia nigra is closely associated with motor system pathways of the basal ganglia.

The human mesencephalon is archipallian in origin, meaning its general architecture is shared with the most ancient of vertebrates. Dopamine produced in the substantia nigra plays a role in motivation and habituation of species from humans to the most elementary animals such as insects.

Corpora quadrigemina

The corpora quadrigemina ("quadruplet bodies") are four solid optic lobes on the dorsal side of cerebral aqueduct, where the superior posterior pair are called the superior colliculi and the inferior posterior pair are called the inferior colliculi. The four solid optic lobes help to decussate several fibres of the optic nerve. However some fibers also show ipsilateral arrangement (i.e. they run parallel on the same side without decussating.) The superior colliculus is involved with saccadic eye movements; while the inferior is a synapsing point for sound information. The trochlear nerve comes out of the posterior surface of the midbrain, below the inferior colliculus.

Cerebral peduncle

The cerebral peduncles are paired structures, present on the ventral side of cerebral aqueduct, and they further carry tegmentum on the dorsal side and cresta or pes on the ventral side, and both of them accommodate the corticospinal tract fibres, from the internal capsule (i.e. ascending + descending tracts = longitudinal tract.) the middle part of cerebral peduncles carry substantia nigra (also called "Black Matter") which is a type of basal nucleus. It is the only part of the brain that carries melanin pigment.

Cross-section through the midbrain

The midbrain is usually sectioned at the level of the superior and inferior colliculi.

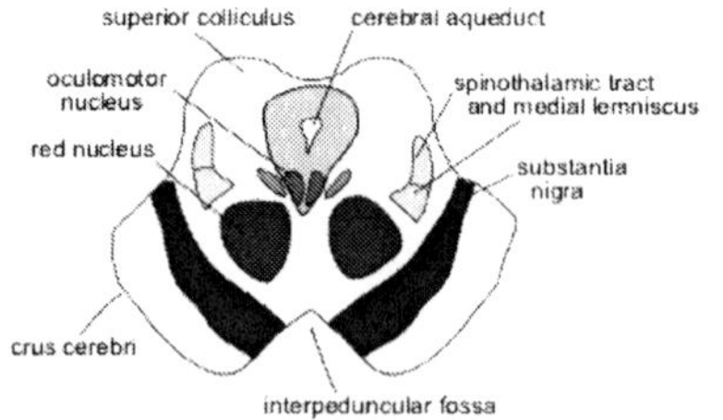

A cross-section at the level of the superior colliculus shows the red nucleus, the nuclei of the oculomotor nerve (and associated Edinger-Westphal nucleus), as well as the substantia nigra.

The substantia nigra is still present at inferior colliculus level. Also apparent are the trochlear nerve nucleus, and the decussation of the superior cerebellar peduncles.

The cerebral aqueduct runs through the midbrain, and is the communication between the third and fourth ventricle.

As a mnemonic the mesencephalic cross-section resembles a bear (or teddy bear) upside down with the two red nuclei as the eyes and the crus cerebri as the ears.

Organization

- mesencephalon
  - tectum
    - inferior colliculi
    - superior colliculi
  - cerebral peduncle
    - midbrain tegmentum
    - crus cerebri
    - substantia nigra

Additional images

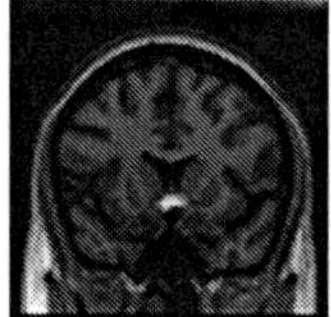

Ventral midbrain

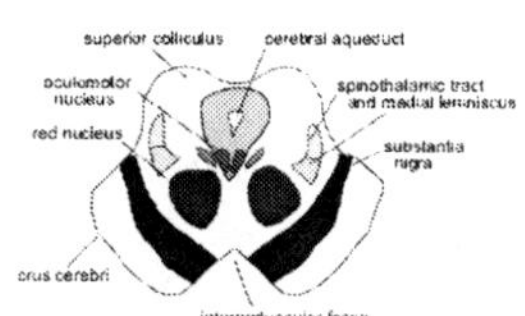

Diagram of the midbrain, sectioned at the level of the superior colliculus

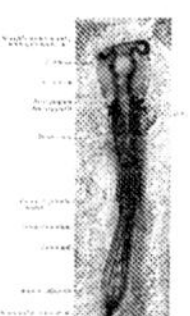

Chick embryo of thirty-three hours' incubation, viewed from the dorsal aspect. X 30.

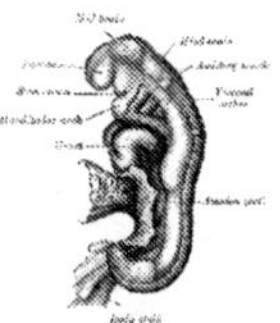

Embryo between eighteen and twenty-one days.

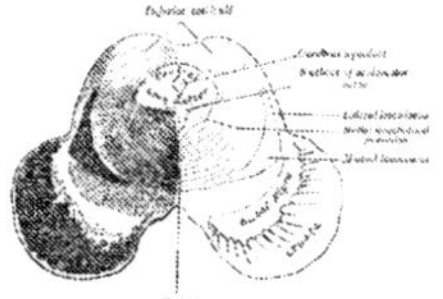
Transverse section of mid-brain at level of inferior colliculi.

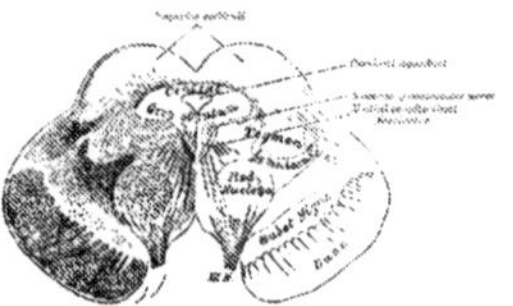
Transverse section of mid-brain at level of superior colliculi.

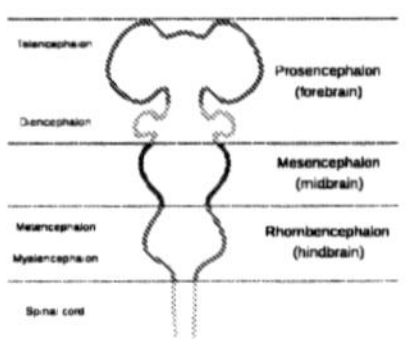

Embryonic brain

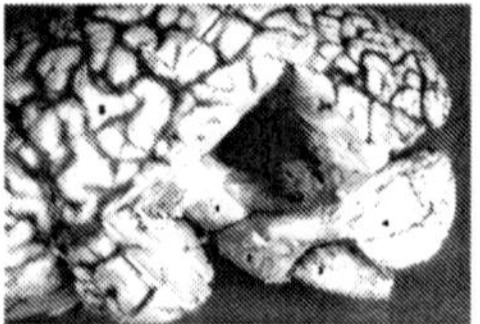
Human cerebrum lateral view

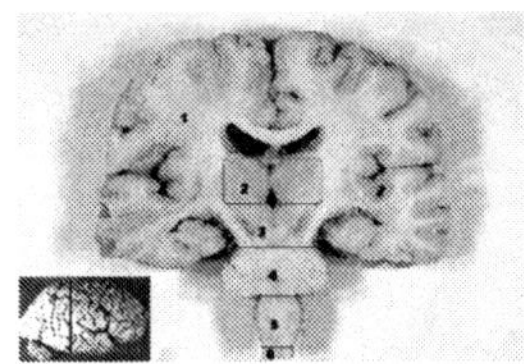
Human brain frontal (coronal) section

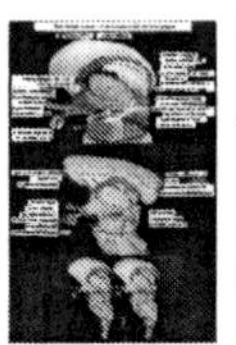
internal view of basal ganglia

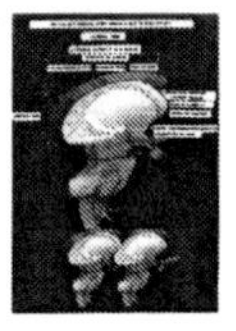
external view of basal ganglia

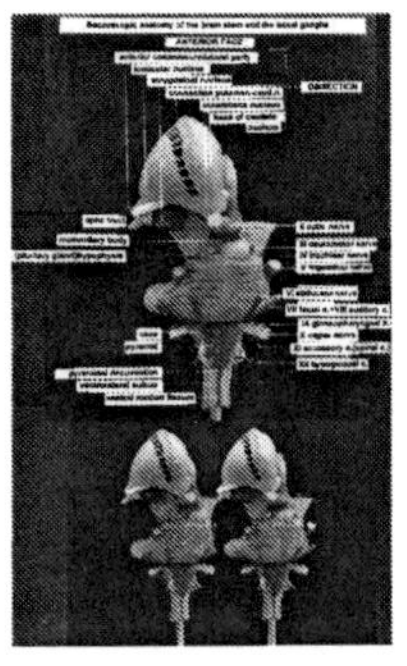
anterior face of brainstem

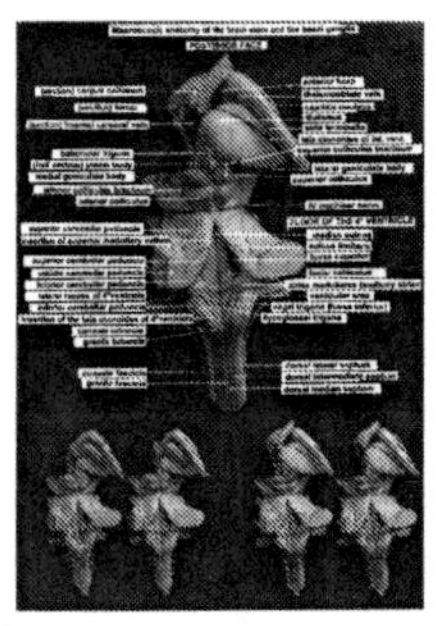
posterior face of brainstem

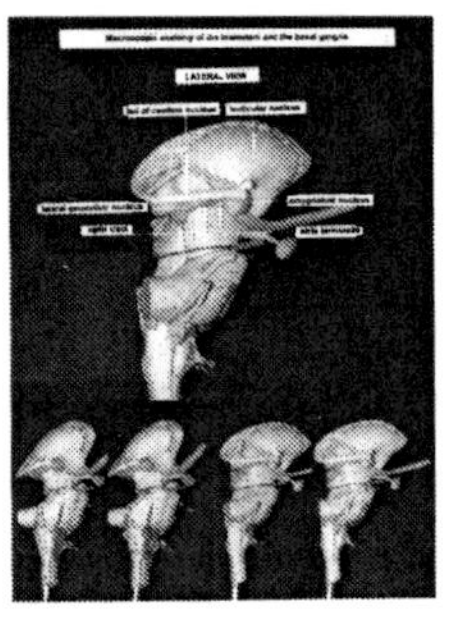
external face of brainstem

See also

- list of regions in the human brain

Medial lemniscus

Medial lemniscus

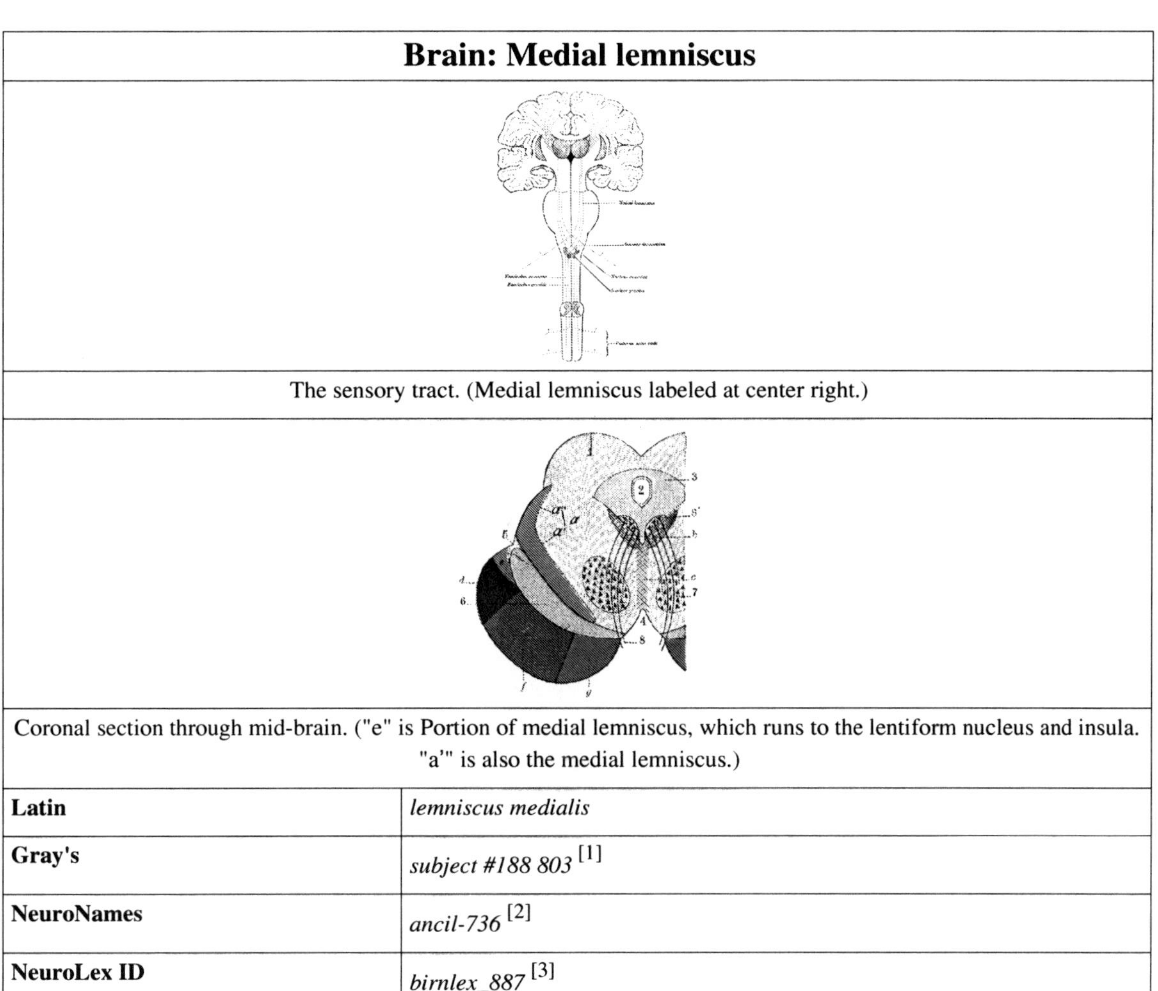

Brain: Medial lemniscus	
The sensory tract. (Medial lemniscus labeled at center right.)	
Coronal section through mid-brain. ("e" is Portion of medial lemniscus, which runs to the lentiform nucleus and insula. "a'" is also the medial lemniscus.)	
Latin	*lemniscus medialis*
Gray's	*subject #188 803* [1]
NeuroNames	*ancil-736* [2]
NeuroLex ID	*birnlex_887* [3]

The **medial lemniscus**, also known as **Reil's band** or **Reil's ribbon**, is a pathway in the brainstem that carries sensory information from the gracile and cuneate nuclei to the thalamus.

Path

After neurons carrying proprioceptive or touch information synapse at the gracile and cuneate nuclei, axons from secondary neurons decussate at the level of the medulla and travel up the brainstem as the medial lemniscus on the contralateral (opposite) side. It is part of the posterior column-medial lemniscus system, which transmits touch, vibration sense, as well as the pathway for proprioception.

The medial lemniscus axons from most of the body synapses in the ventral posterolateral nucleus of the thalamus, at the level of the mamillary bodies. Sensory axons transmitting information from the head and neck via the trigeminal nerve synapse at the ventral posteromedial nucleus of the thalamus.

Location of the medial lemniscus through the brainstem

- The cuneate and gracile nuclei reside at the *closed (lower) medulla*, so the lemniscus isn't formed at this level. Fibres from these nuclei will pass to the contralateral side of the brainstem, as the internal arcuate fibres.
- At the *open medulla* (further up the brainstem), the medial lemniscus contains axons from the trigeminal nerve (which supplies the head region), as well as the arms and legs. It sits very close to the midline, at the same orientation of the midline, with head fibres more dorsal (closer to the back), towards the fourth ventricle.
- By *mid-pons*, the medial lemniscus has rotated. Fibres from the head are medial, fibres from the leg are lateral.
- The orientation in the *midbrain* is similar to that in the pons.

See also

- Posterior column-medial lemniscus pathway

Additional images

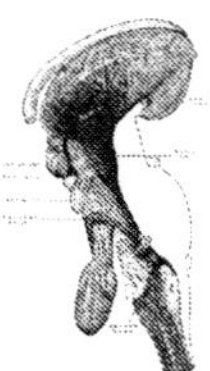

Deep dissection of brain-stem. Lateral view.

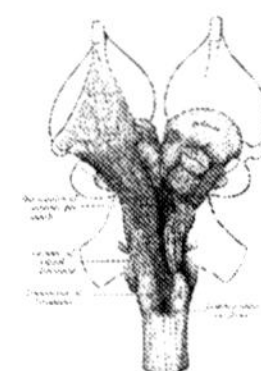

Deep dissection of brain-stem. Ventral view.

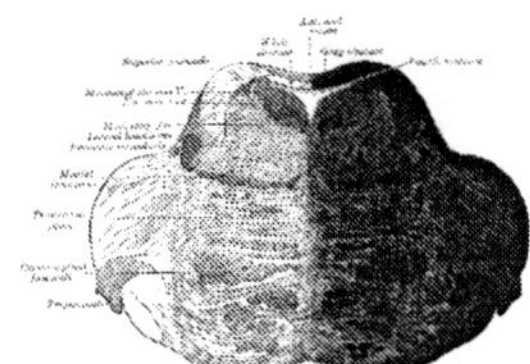

Coronal section of the pons, at its upper part.

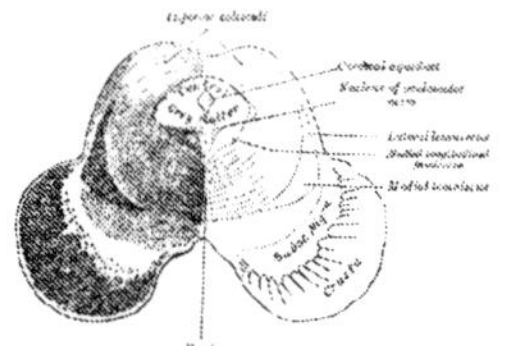

Transverse section of mid-brain at level of inferior colliculi.

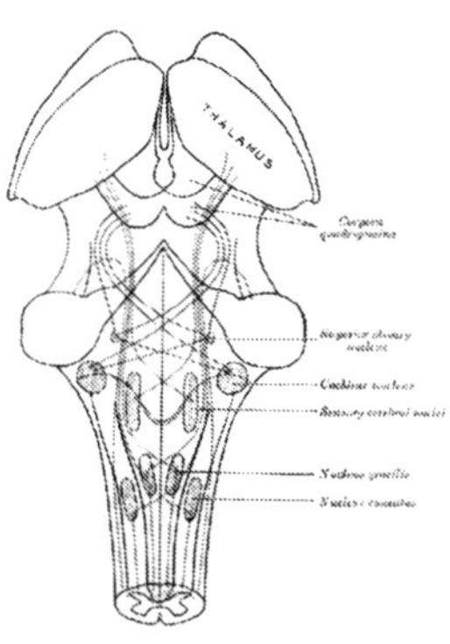

Scheme showing the course of the fibers of the lemniscus; medial lemniscus in blue, lateral in red.

External links

- Brainstem at UWisc *04NGNC* [4]
- BrainMaps at UCDavis *medial lemniscus* [5]

Nucleus ambiguus

Nucleus ambiguus

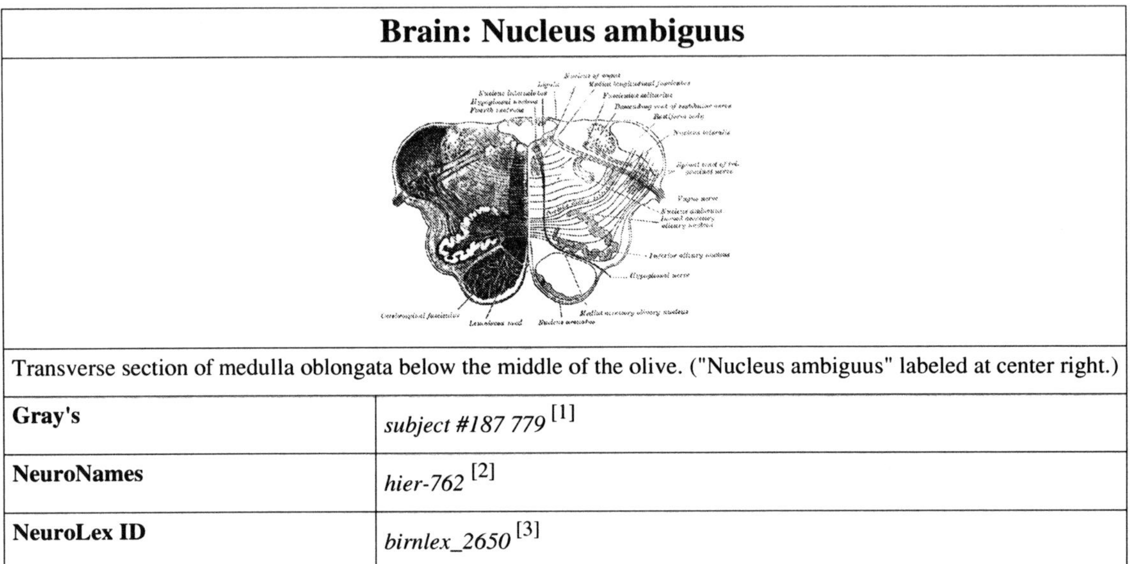

Brain: Nucleus ambiguus	
Transverse section of medulla oblongata below the middle of the olive. ("Nucleus ambiguus" labeled at center right.)	
Gray's	*subject #187 779* [1]
NeuroNames	*hier-762* [2]
NeuroLex ID	*birnlex_2650* [3]

The **nucleus ambiguus** (literally "ambiguous nucleus") is a region of histologically disparate cells located just dorsal (posterior) to the inferior olivary nucleus in the lateral portion of the upper (rostral) medulla. It receives upper motor neuron innervation directly via the corticobulbar tract.

This nucleus gives rise to the visceral efferent motor fibers of the vagus nerve (CN X) terminating in the laryngeal and pharyngeal muscles, as well as to the efferent motor fibers of the glossopharyngeal nerve (CN IX) terminating in the stylopharyngeus.

Areas supplied

The muscles supplied by the vagus (included with this is the cranial part of the accessory nerve), such as levator veli palatini, are also necessary to swallow properly through integration by the nucleus of the solitary tract. The vagus also supplies the upper part of the esophagus, and other parts of the pharynx and larynx.

As well as motor neurons, the nucleus ambiguus in its "external formation" contains cholinergic preganglionic parasympathetic neurons for the heart. These neurons are cardioinhibitory This cardioinhibitory effect is one of the means by which quick changes in blood pressure are achieved by the central nervous system (the primary means being changes in sympathetic nervous system activity, which constricts arterioles and makes the heart pump faster and harder). That is, through integrated and antagonistic system with sympathetic outflow from the vasomotor center of the brainstem, the parasympathetic outflow arising from the nucleus ambiguus and dorsal motor nucleus of the vagus nerve acts to decrease cardiac activity in response to fast increases in blood pressure. The external formation of the nucleus ambiguus also sends bronchoconstrictor fibers to the bronchopulmonary system, which can produce reflexive decreases in pulmonary bronchial airflow. The pathophysiologic relevance of this system, which may act in concert with the cardioinhibitory system, is poorly understood, but likely plays a role in bronchospastic diseases like COPD/emphysema (in which inhaled anticholinergic medications such as Spiriva/tiotropium or ipratropium are standard-of-care treatment) and asthma, particularly for exercise-related asthma exacerbations, which may have a component of autonomic dysregulation.

Additional images

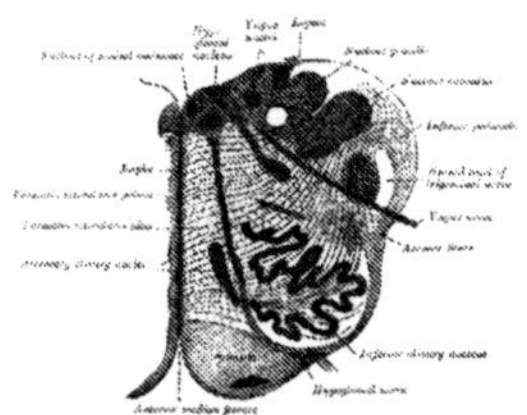

Section of the medulla oblongata at about the middle of the olive.

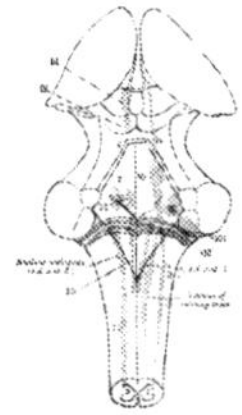

The cranial nerve nuclei schematically represented; dorsal view. Motor nuclei in red; sensory in blue.

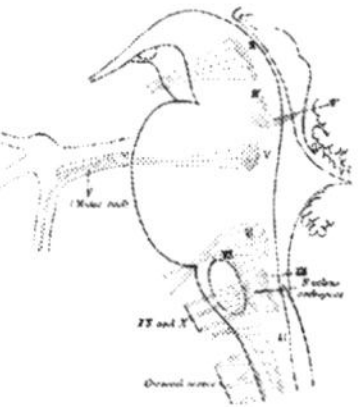

Nuclei of origin of cranial motor nerves schematically represented; lateral view.

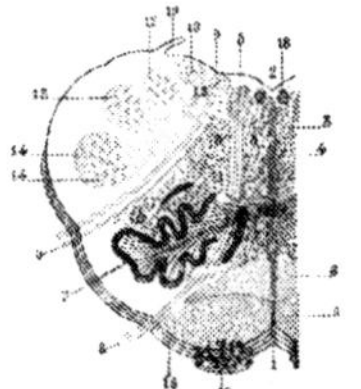

The formatio reticularis of the medulla oblongata, shown by a transverse section passing through the middle of the olive.

External links

- Medical Neurosciences [4] discuss the nucleus ambiguus.
- *-1664090053* [5] at GPnotebook

Medial longitudinal fasciculus

Medial longitudinal fasciculus

<table>
<tr><th colspan="2">Brain: Medial longitudinal fasciculus</th></tr>
<tr><td colspan="2">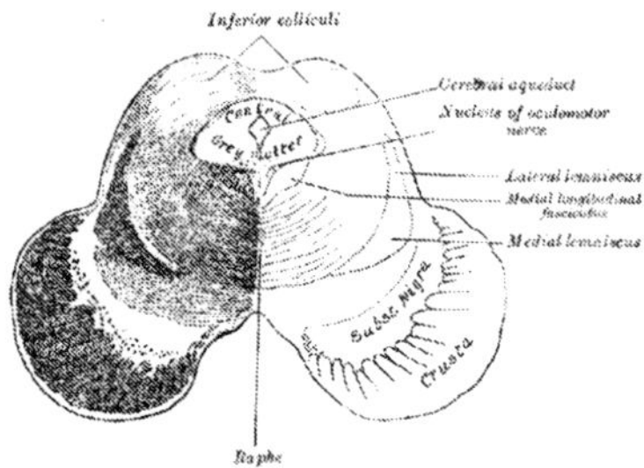
</td></tr>
<tr><td colspan="2">Transverse section of mid-brain at level of inferior colliculi. (Medial longitudinal fasciculus labeled at center right.)</td></tr>
<tr><td colspan="2">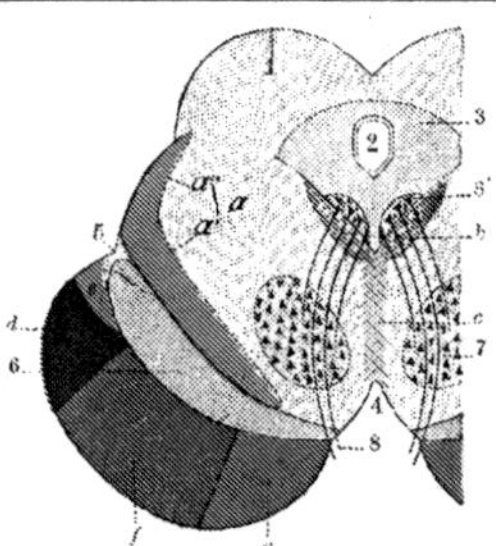</td></tr>
<tr><td colspan="2">Coronal section through mid-brain.
1. Corpora quadrigemina.
2. Cerebral aqueduct.
3. Central gray stratum.
4. Interpeduncular space.
5. Sulcus lateralis.
6. Substantia nigra.
7. Red nucleus of tegmentum.
8. Oculomotor nerve, with 8', its nucleus of origin. a. Lemniscus (in blue) with a' the medial lemniscus and a" the lateral lemniscus. b. Medial longitudinal fasciculus. c. Raphé. d. Temporopontine fibers. e. Portion of medial lemniscus, which runs to the lentiform nucleus and insula. f. Cerebrospinal fibers. g. Frontopontine fibers.</td></tr>
<tr><td>Latin</td><td>fasciculus longitudinalis medialis</td></tr>
<tr><td>Gray's</td><td>subject #188 803 [1]</td></tr>
<tr><td>NeuroNames</td><td>ancil-743 [1]</td></tr>
</table>

The **medial longitudinal fasciculus** (MLF) is a pair of crossed fiber tracts (group of axons), one on each side of the brainstem. These bundles of axons are situated near the midline of the brainstem and are composed of both ascending and descending fibers that arise from a number of sources and terminate in different areas.

Function

The MLF carries information about the direction that the eyes should move.

It yokes the cranial nerve nuclei III (Oculomotor nerve), IV (Trochlear nerve) and VI (Abducens nerve) together, and integrates movements directed by the gaze centers (frontal eye field) and information about head movement (from cranial nerve VIII, Vestibulocochlear nerve). It is an integral component of saccadic eye movements as well as vestibulo-ocular and optokinetic reflexes.

It also carries the descending tectospinal tract and medial vestibulospinal tracts into the cervical spinal cord, and innervates some muscles of the neck and upper limbs.

Inputs

The descending MLF mainly arises from the medial Vestibular nucleus (VN) and is thought to be involved in the maintenance of gaze. This is achieved by inputs to the VN from

1. the Vestibulocochlear (8th cranial) nerve about head movements,
2. gain adjustments from the flocculus of the cerebellum,
3. head and neck propioceptors and foot and ankle muscle spindle, via the fastigial nucleus.

Descending fibers can also arise from the superior colliculus in the rostral midbrain for visual reflexes, the accessory occulomotor nuclei in the rostral midbrain for visual tracking, and the pontine reticular formation, which facilitates extensor muscle tone. Ascending tracts arise from the Vestibular nucleus (VN) and terminate in the III, IV and VI nuclei, which are important for visual tracking.

Pathology

Lesions of the MLF produce internuclear ophthalmoplegia and can be a presenting symptom of multiple sclerosis,where it presents as nystagmus and occasionally diplopia. These lesions cause damage to the ipsilateral (same side) eye.

History

In 1846 neurologist Benedict Stilling first referred to what is now known as the MLF as the *acusticus*, followed by Theodor Meynert in 1872 calling it *posterior*. But in 1891, Heinrich Schutz chose the name *dorsal* to describe the longitudinal bundle, "for brevity's sake". This name stuck despite other authors attempting further renaming (Ramon y Cajal's *periependymal* in 1904, Theodor Ziehen's *nubecula dorsalis* in 1913). But finally, it was Wilhelm His, Sr. who changed the name to *medial* for the sake of the Basle nomenclature to end the confusion.

Additional images

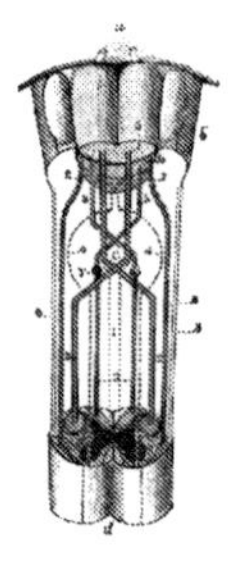

Decussation of pyramids.

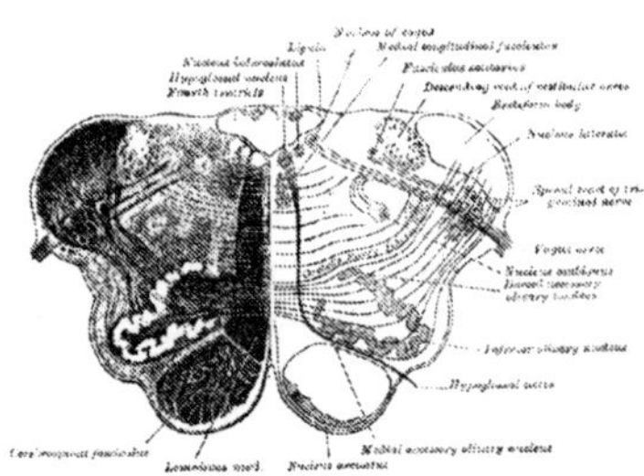

Transverse section of medulla oblongata below the middle of the olive.

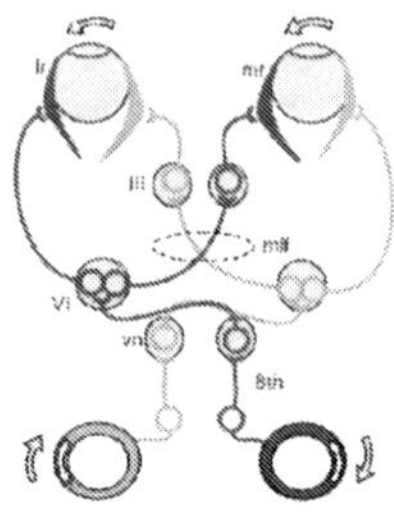

Vestibulo-ocular reflex

External links

- *Medial+longitudinal+fasciculus* [2] at eMedicine Dictionary
- Atlas of anatomy at UMich *n2a4p4* [3] - "Brainstem, Cranial Nerve Nuclei, Sagittal Section, Medial View"
- http://isc.temple.edu/neuroanatomy/lab/atlas/papc/

Lateral lemniscus

Lateral lemniscus

Brain: Lateral lemniscus	
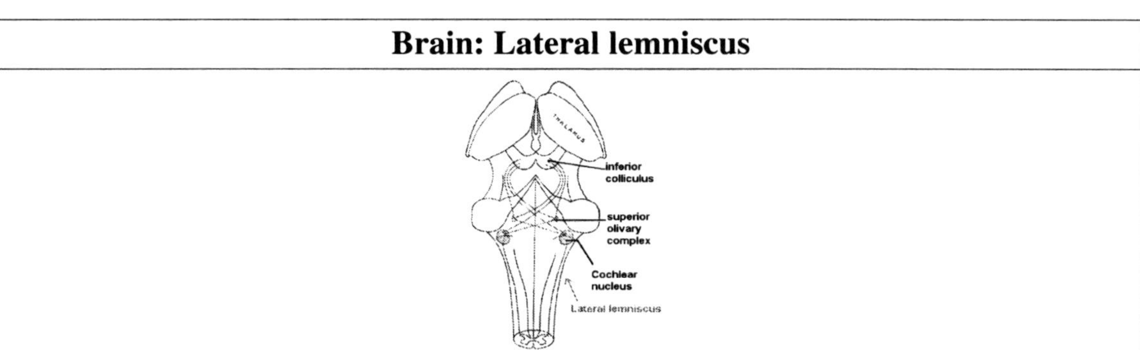	
Lateral lemniscus in red, as it connects the cochlear nucleus, superior olivary nucleus and the inferior colliculus. Seen from behind.	
Figure 1: Arrangement of the lateral lemniscus, showing the tract and nuclei. Dorsal nucleus of the lateral lemniscus (DNLL), Intermediate nucleus of the lateral lemniscus (INLL), ventral nucleus of the lateral lemniscus (VNLL).	
Latin	*lemniscus lateralis*
Gray's	*subject #188 805* [1]
NeuroNames	*hier-605* [2]
NeuroLex ID	*birnlex_774* [3]

The **lateral lemniscus** is a tract of axons in the brainstem that carries information about sound from the cochlear nucleus to various brainstem nuclei and ultimately the contralateral inferior colliculus of the midbrain. Three distinct, primarily inhibitory, cellular groups are located interspersed within these fibers, and are thus named the nuclei of the lateral lemniscus.

Connections

The brainstem nuclei include:

- the superior olive
- the intermediate nucleus of the lateral lemniscus (INLL)
- the ventral nucleus of the lateral lemniscus (VNLL)
- the dorsal nucleus of the lateral lemniscus (DNLL)

Fibers leaving these brainstem nuclei ascending to the inferior colliculus rejoin the lateral lemniscus. In that sense, this is not a 'lemniscus' in the true sense of the word (second order, decussated sensory axons), as there is third (and out of the lateral superior olive, fourth) order information coming out of some of these brainstem nuclei.

The lateral lemniscus is located where the cochlear nuclei and the pontine reticular formation (PRF) crossover. The PRF descends the reticulospinal tract where it innervates motor neurons and spinal interneurons. It is the main auditory tract in the brainstem that connects the superior olivary complex (SOC) with the inferior colliculus (IC). The dorsal cochlear nucleus (DCN) has input from the LL and output to the contralateral LL via the ipsilateral and contralateral Dorsal Acoustic Stria.

There are three small nuclei on each of the lateral lemnisci: the ventral, dorsal, and the intermediate. The two lemnisci communicate via the commissural fibers of Probst.

Nuclei of the Lateral Lemniscus

The function of the lateral lemniscus is not known; however it has good temporal resolution compared to other cells higher than the cochlear nuclei and is sensitive to both timing and amplitude changes in sound. It is also involved in the acoustic startle reflex; the most likely region for this being the VNLL.

DNLL

The cells of the DNLL respond best to bilateral inputs, and have onset and complexity tuned sustained responses. The nucleus is primarily GABAergic, and projects bilaterally to the inferior colliculus, and contralaterally to the DNLL, with different populations of cells projecting to each IC.

In rat, the DNLL has a prominent columnar organization. Nearly all neurons are stained for GABA, especially in the central part of the nucleus, and the remaining GABA negative cells are interspersed with the positive, and often stain for glycine. Two populations of GABA+ cells are visible: larger, lightly stained cells that project to the contralateral IC, and smaller, darker stained cells that project ipsilaterally. GABAergic axon terminals form dense groups surrounded by GABA-lemniscal fibers throughout the nucleus, and synapse on both somata and in the neuropil. Glycinergic axon terminals, on the other hand, are more finely localized, with the majority of recipient neurons located laterally in the nucleus.

INLL

INLL also has little spontaneous activity and broad tuning curves. The temporal responses are significantly different from cells of the VNLL.

VNLL

Sound in the contralateral ear leads to the strongest responses in the VNLL, which deals with some temporary processing. The VNLL may also be essential to the IC's decoding of amplitude modulated sounds.

VNLL cells have little spontaneous activity, broad and moderately complex tuning curves; they have both phasic and tonic responses and are involved in temporal processing.

Inputs and outputs to nuclei

The table below shows that each of the nuclei have a complicated arrangement of ipsilateral and contralateral afferent inputs and outputs.

Nucleus	Input		Output	
	Contralateral	Ipsilateral	Contralateral	Ipsilateral
VNLL	Anterior and posterior ventral cochlear nuclei	Medial nucleus of the trapezoid body		Inferior Colliculus DNLL
INLL	Anterior and posterior Ventral Cochlear Nucleus	Medial nucleus of the trapezoid body		Medial Geniculate body Inferior Colliculus
DNLL	Anterior Ventral Cochlear nucleus (and Bilateral)	Medial superior Olivary Nucleus Lateral Superior Olivary Nucleus (and Bilateral)	DNLL Inferior Colliculus Mid brain reticular formation Superior Olivary Complex	Inferior Colliculus Medial Geniculate Body Mid brain reticular formation Superior Olivary Complex

Additional images

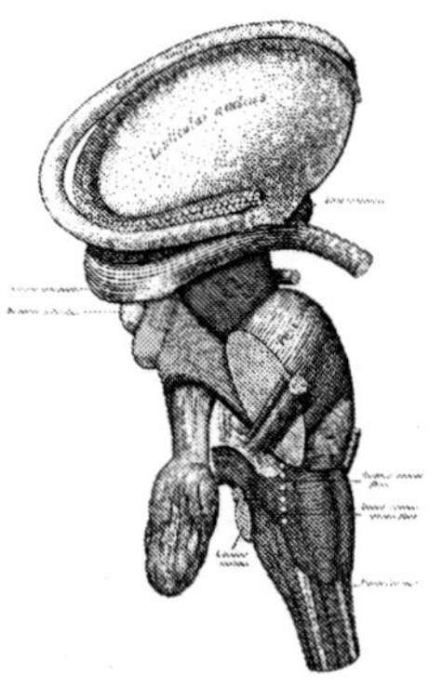
Dissection of brain-stem. Lateral view.

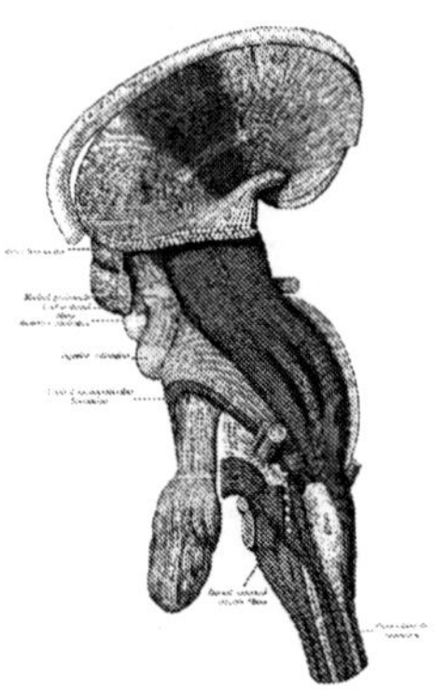
Deep dissection of brain-stem. Lateral view.

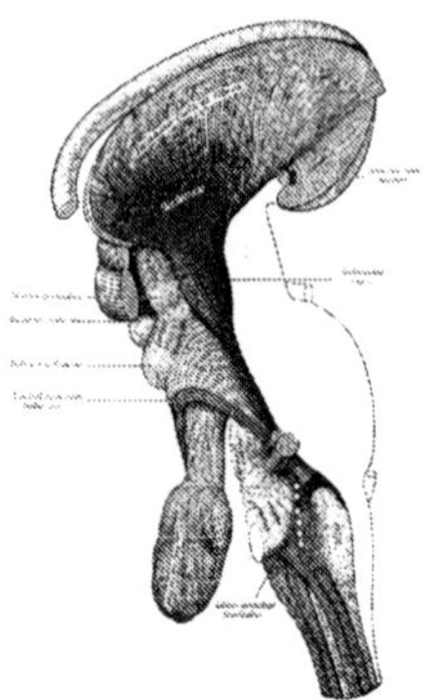
Deep dissection of brain-stem. Lateral view.

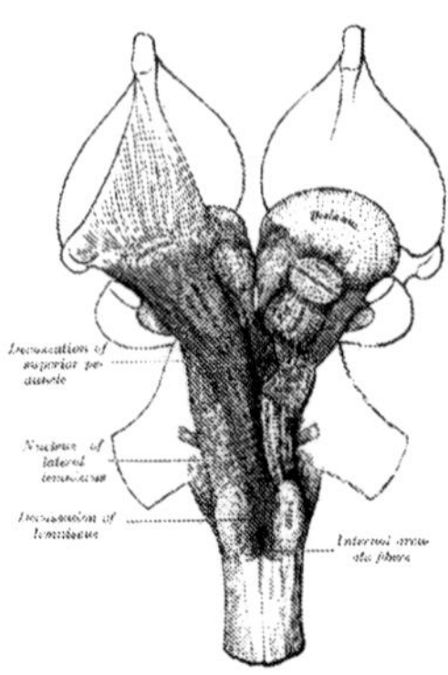
Deep dissection of brain-stem. Ventral view.

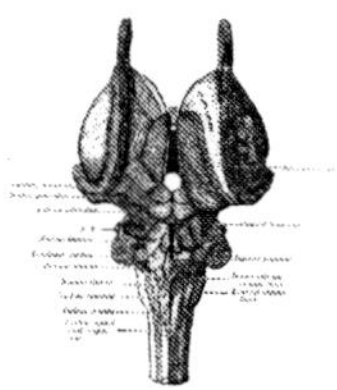
Dissection of brain-stem. Dorsal view.

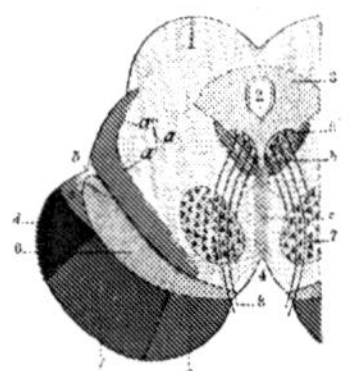
Coronal section through mid-brain.

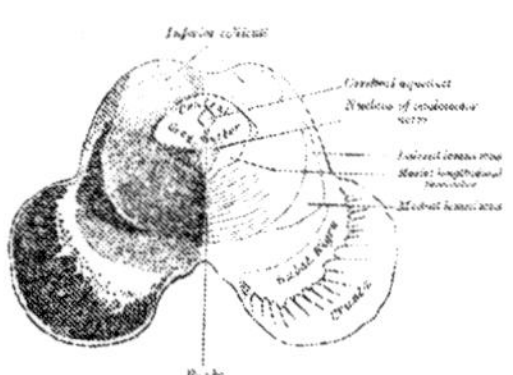
Transverse section of mid-brain at level of inferior colliculi.

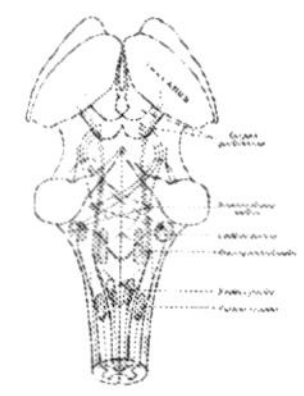
Scheme showing the course of the fibers of the lemniscus; medial lemniscus in blue, lateral in red.

Locus coeruleus

Locus coeruleus

Brain: Locus coeruleus	
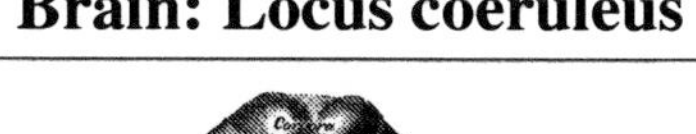 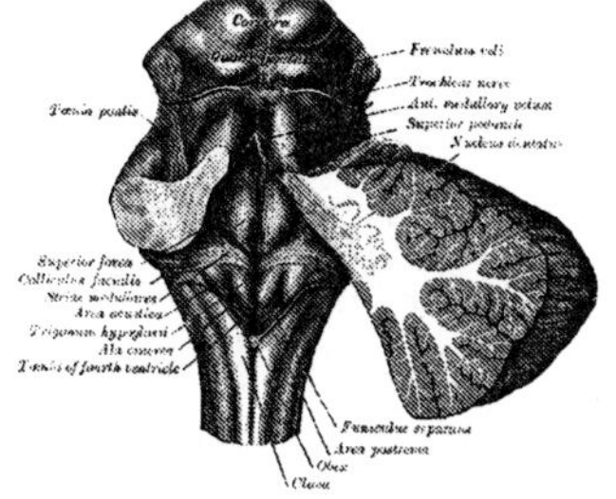	
Rhomboid fossa. (Locus coeruleus not labeled, but region is very near colliculus facialis, which is labeled at center left.)	
Latin	*locus caeruleus*
Gray's	*subject #187 778* [1]
NeuroNames	*hier-578* [2]
NeuroLex ID	*birnlex_905* [3]

The **Locus coeruleus**, also spelled **locus caeruleus**, is a nucleus in the brain stem involved with physiological responses to stress and panic. It was discovered in the 18th century by Félix Vicq-d'Azyr.

Its name is derived from the Latin words "coeruleus" and "locus". Literally, this means "the blue spot", a name derived from its azure appearance in unstained brain tissue. The color is due to light scattering from melanin in noradrenergic nerve cell bodies. *Caeruleus* is the classical Latin spelling, but *coeruleus*, a more archaic form, is the more common spelling. The spelling *ceruleus*, formed by contraction of the digraph ae or oe into e, is an American English form.

Anatomy

The locus coeruleus (or "LC") is in the dorsal wall of the rostral pons in the lateral floor of the fourth ventricle. This nucleus is the principal site for brain synthesis of noradrenaline (or "NA", also known as norepinephrine or "NE"). It is composed of mostly medium-size neurons. Melanin granules inside the neurons of the LC contribute to its blue color. Thus, it is also known as the nucleus pigmentosus pontis, meaning "heavily pigmented nucleus of the pons." The neuromelanin is formed by the polymerization of noradrenaline and is analogous to the black dopamine-based neuromelanin in the substantia nigra.

In adult humans (19-78) the locus coeruleus has 22,000 to 51,000 total pigmented neurons that range in size between 31,000 to 60, 000 μm^3.

Connections

The projections of this nucleus reach far and wide. For example, they innervate the spinal cord, the brain stem, cerebellum, hypothalamus, the thalamic relay nuclei, the amygdala, the basal telencephalon, and the cortex. The norepinephrine from the LC has an excitatory effect on most of the brain, mediating arousal and priming the brain's neurons to be activated by stimuli.

As an important homeostatic control center of the body, the locus coeruleus receives afferents from the hypothalamus. The cingulate gyrus and the amygdala also innervate the LC, allowing emotional pain and stressors to trigger noradrenergic responses. The cerebellum and afferents from the raphe nuclei also project to the LC, particularly the raphe pontis and raphe dorsalis.

The locus coeruleus receives inputs from a number of other brain regions, primarily:

- Medial prefrontal cortex, whose connection is constant, excitatory, and increases in strength with raised activity levels in the subject
- Nucleus paragigantocellularis, which integrates autonomic and environmental stimuli
- Nucleus prepositus hypoglossi, which is involved in gaze
- Lateral hypothalamus, which releases orexin, which, as well as its other functions, is excitatory in the locus coeruleus.

Function

The locus coeruleus may figure in clinical depression, panic disorder, and anxiety. Some antidepressant medications including reboxetine, venlafaxine, and bupropion, as well as ADHD medication atomoxetine, are believed to act on neurons in this area. This area of the brain is also intimately involved in REM sleep.

In stress

The locus coeruleus is responsible for mediating many of the sympathetic effects during stress. The locus coeruleus is activated by stress, and will respond by increasing norepinephrine secretion, which in turn will alter cognitive function (through the prefrontal cortex), increase motivation (through nucleus accumbens), activate the hypothalamic-pituitary-adrenal axis, and increase the sympathetic discharge/inhibit parasympathetic tone (through the brainstem). Specific to the activation of the hypothalamo-pituitary adrenal axis, norepinephrine will stimulate the secretion of corticotropin-releasing factor from the hypothalamus, which induces adrenocorticotropic hormone release from the anterior pituitary and subsequent cortisol synthesis in the adrenal glands. Norepinephrine released from locus coeruleus will feedback to inhibit its production, and corticotropin-releasing hormone will feedback to inhibit its production, while positively feeding to the locus coeruleus to increase norepinephrine production.

The LC's role in cognitive function in relation to stress is complex and multi-modal. Norepinephrine released from the LC can act on $\alpha 2$ receptors to increase working memory, or an excess of NE may decrease working memory by binding to the lower affinity $\alpha 1$ receptors.

In opiate withdrawal

Rett syndrome

The genetic defect of the transcriptional regulator MECP2 is responsible for Rett syndrome. A MeCP2 deficiency has been associated to catecholaminergic dysfunctions related to autonomic and sympathoadrenergic system in mouse models of RTT. The Locus Coeruleus is the major source of noradrenergic innervation in the brain and sends widespread connections to rostral (cerebral cortex, hippocampus, hypothalamus) and caudal (cerebellum, brainstem nuclei) brain areas and . Indeed, an alteration of this structure could contribute to several symptoms observed in Mecp2-deficient mice. Changes in the electrophysiological properties of cells in the locus ceruleus were shown. These Locus Coeruleus cell changes include hyperexcitability and decreased functioning of its noradrenergic innervation.. Interestingly, a reduction of the tyrosine hydroxylase (Th) mRNA level, the rate-limiting enzyme in catecholamine synthesis, was detected in the whole pons of Mecp2-null male as well as in adult heterozygous female mice. Using immunoquantification techniques, a decrease of TH protein staining level, number of locus coeruleus TH-expressing neurons and density of dendritic arborization surrounding the structure was shown in symptomatic Mecp2-deficient mice. However, locus coeruleus cells are not dying but are more likely losing their fully mature phenotype since no apoptotic neurons in the pons were detected. Researchers have concluded that "Because these neurons are a pivotal source of norepinephrine throughout the brainstem and forebrain and are involved in the regulation of diverse functions disrupted in Rett syndrome, such as respiration and cognition, we hypothesize that the locus ceruleus is a critical site at which loss of MECP2 results in CNS dysfunction. Restoration of normal locus ceruleus function may therefore be of potential therapeutic value in the treatment of Rett Syndrome. This could explain why a norepinephrine reuptake inhibitor (desipramine, DMI) which enhance the extracellular NE levels at all noradrenergic synapses could ameliorates some symptoms in a mouse model of Rett Syndrome.

Alzheimer's Disease

There is up to 70% loss of locus ceruleus neurons in Alzheimer's Disease. Mouse models of Alzheimer's disease show accelerated progression after chemical destruction of the locus ceruleus The norepinephrine from locus ceruleus cells in addition to its neurotransmitter role locally defuses from "varicosities". As such it provides an endogenous antiinflammatory agent in the microenvironment around the neurons, glial cells, and blood vessels in the neocortex and hippocampus. It has been shown that norepinephrine stimulates mouse microglia to suppress Aβ-induced production of cytokines and their phagocytosis of Aβ. This suggests that degeneration of the locus ceruleus might be responsible for increased Aβ deposition in AD brains.

See also

- Raphe nucleus
- Substantia nigra
- Reticular formation

External links

- "A Lecture, Higher Brain Function: Activation of the Brain and Levels of Consciousness" [4] at East Tennessee State University
- BrainMaps at UCDavis *locus coeruleus* [5]
- Diagram [6] at University of Texas at Austin
- Diagram [7] at University of Virginia
- http://www2.umdnj.edu/~neuro/studyaid/Practical2000/Q45.htm

Fourth ventricle

Fourth ventricle

Brain: Fourth ventricle

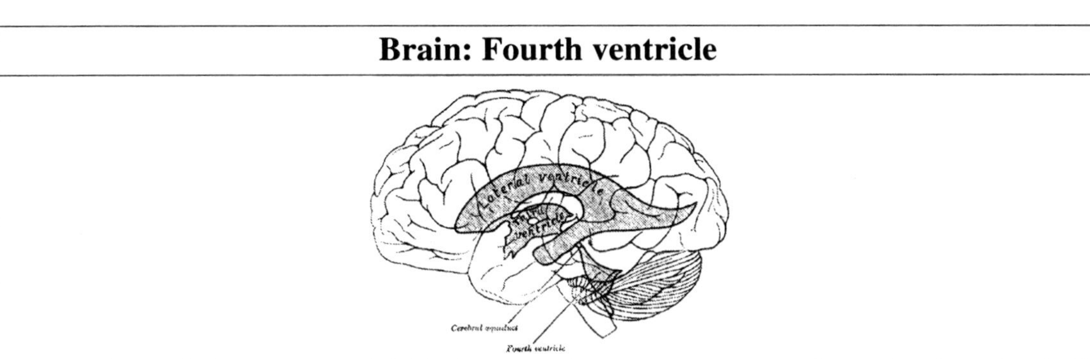

Scheme showing relations of the ventricles to the surface of the brain. (Fourth ventricle labeled at bottom center.)

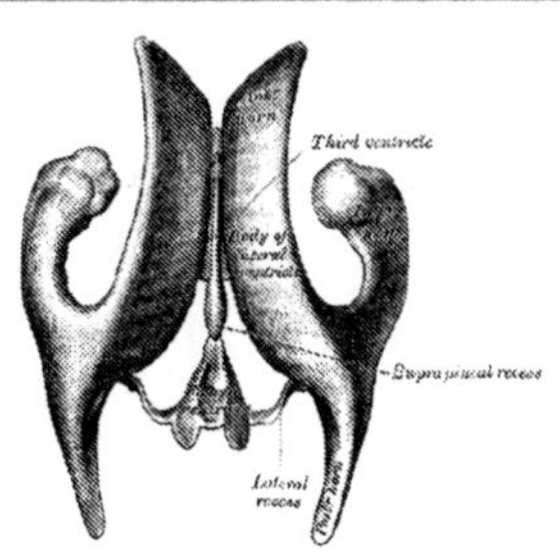

Drawing of a cast of the ventricular cavities, viewed from above. (Fourth ventricle visible at bottom center.)

Latin	*ventriculus quartus*	
Gray's	*subject #187 797* [1]	
NeuroNames	*hier-617* [2]	
MeSH	*Fourth+Ventricle* [3]	

The **fourth ventricle** is one of the four connected fluid-filled cavities within the human brain. These cavities, known collectively as the ventricular system, consist of the left and right lateral ventricles, the third ventricle, and the fourth ventricle. The fourth ventricle extends from the cerebral aqueduct (*aqueduct of Sylvius*) to the obex, and is filled with cerebrospinal fluid (CSF).

The fourth ventricle has a characteristic diamond shape in cross-sections of the human brain. It is located within the pons or in the upper part of the medulla. CSF entering the fourth ventricle through the cerebral aqueduct can exit to the subarachnoid space of the spinal cord through two lateral foramina of Luschka (singular: *foramen of Luschka*) and a single, midline foramen of Magendie (see List of human anatomical parts named after people).

Roof and floor

The fourth ventricle has a "roof" dorsally and a "floor" ventrally. The roof of the fourth ventricle is formed by the cerebellum (superior and inferior medullary vela), the floor by the rhomboid fossa, and the side "walls" formed by the cerebellar peduncles. Among the prominent features of the floor of the fourth ventricle are the:

- **facial colliculus**: formed by the internal part of the facial nerve as it loops around the abducens nucleus in the lower pons;
- **sulcus limitans**: which represents the border between the alar plate and the basal plate of the developing neural tube;
- **obex**: represents the caudal tip of the fourth ventricle; the obex is also a marker for the level of the foramen magnum of the skull and therefore is a marker for the imaginary dividing line between the medulla and spinal cord.

Development

The fourth ventricle, similarly to other parts of the ventricular system of the brain, develops from the central canal of the neural tube. Specifically, the fourth ventricle originates from the portion of the tube that is present in the developing rhombencephalon. During the first trimester of pregnancy central canal expands into lateral, third and fourth ventricles, connected by thinner channels. In lateral ventricles specialized areas- choroid plexuses appear, which produce cerebrospinal fluid. If its production is bigger than resorption or its circulation is blocked- the enlargement of the ventricles may appear and cause a hydrocephalus. Fetal lateral ventricles may be diagnosed using linear or planar measurements.

Additional images

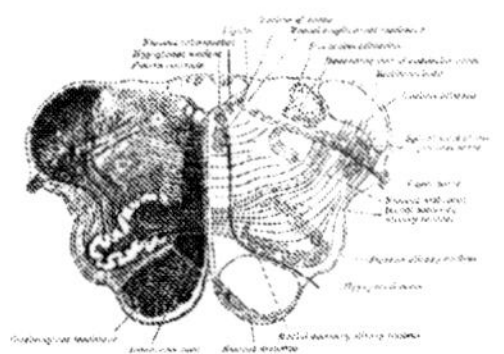
Transverse section of medulla oblongata below the middle of the olive.

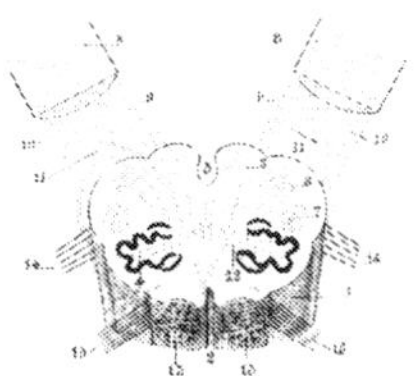
Diagram showing the course of the arcuate fibers.

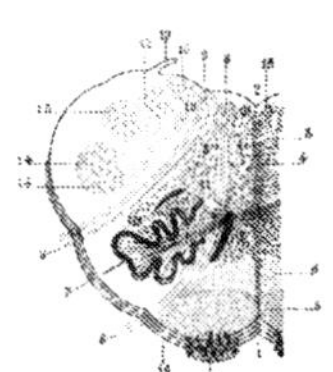
The formatio reticularis of the medulla oblongata, shown by a transverse section passing through the middle of the olive.

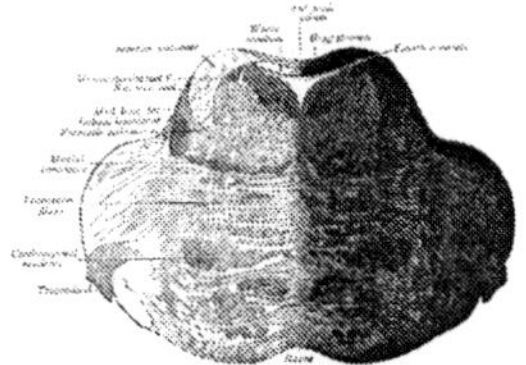
Coronal section of the pons, at its upper part.

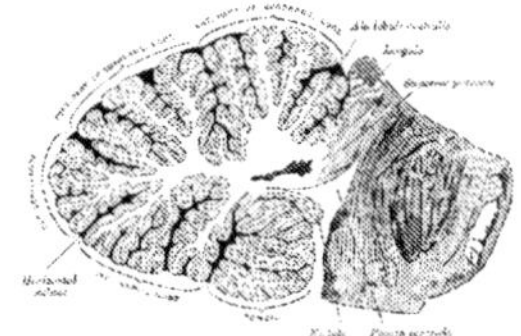
Sagittal section of the cerebellum, near the junction of the vermis with the hemisphere.

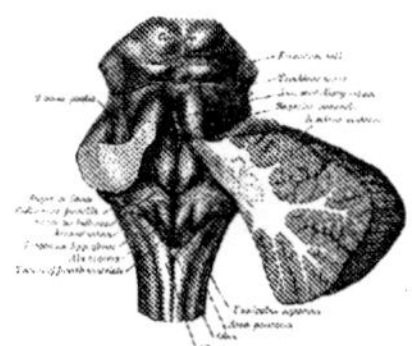
Rhomboid fossa.

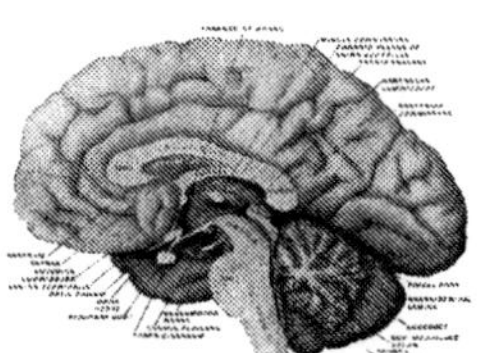
Mesal aspect of a brain sectioned in the median sagittal plane.

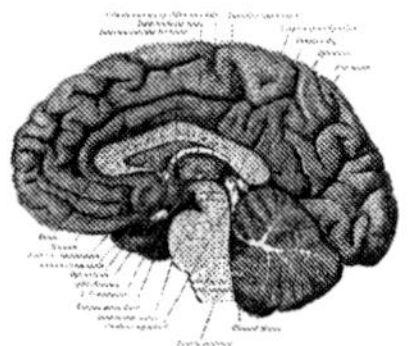
Median sagittal section of brain.

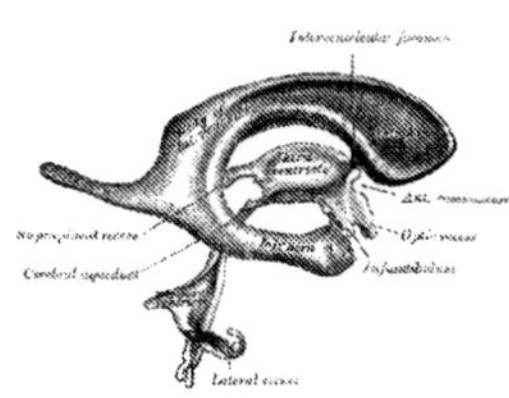
Drawing of a cast of the ventricular cavities, viewed from the side.

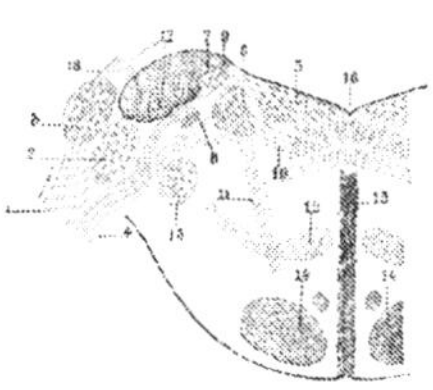
Terminal nuclei of the vestibular nerve, with their upper connections.

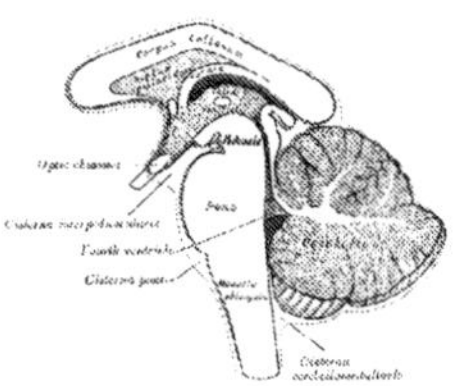
Diagram showing the positions of the three principal subarachnoid cisternæ.

External links

- Atlas of anatomy at UMich *n2a8p1* [4] - "Fourth Ventricle, Sagittal Section, Medial View"
- BrainMaps at UCDavis *fourth%20ventricle* [5]
- *fourth+ventricle* [6] at eMedicine Dictionary
- Roche Lexicon - illustrated navigator, at Elsevier *13048.000-3* [7]

Cuneate nucleus

Cuneate nucleus

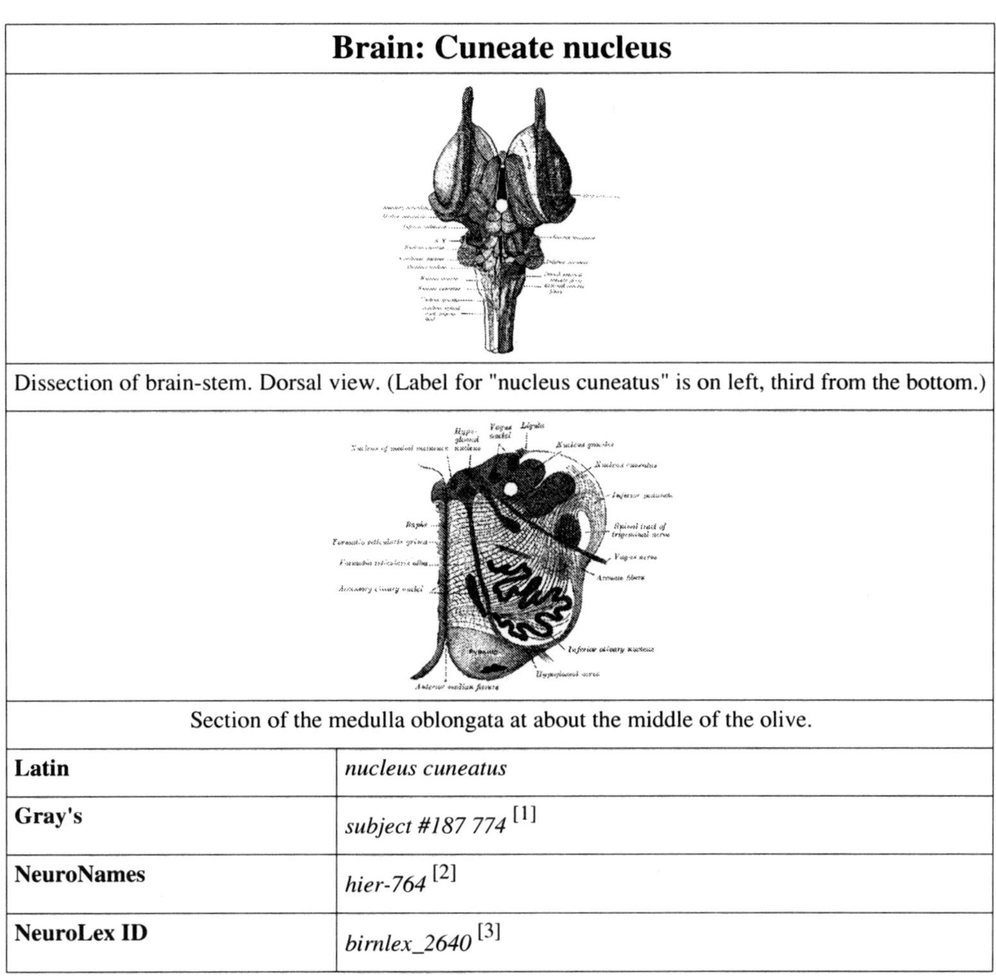

Brain: Cuneate nucleus	
Dissection of brain-stem. Dorsal view. (Label for "nucleus cuneatus" is on left, third from the bottom.)	
Section of the medulla oblongata at about the middle of the olive.	
Latin	*nucleus cuneatus*
Gray's	*subject #187 774* [1]
NeuroNames	*hier-764* [2]
NeuroLex ID	*birnlex_2640* [3]

One of the dorsal column nuclei, the **cuneate nucleus** is a wedge-shaped nucleus in the closed part of the medulla oblongata. It contains cells that give rise to the **cuneate tubercle**, visible on the posterior aspect of the medulla. It lies laterally to the gracile nucleus and medial to the spinal trigeminal nucleus in the medulla.

Function

The cuneate nucleus is part of dorsal column-medial lemniscus system, carrying fine touch and proprioceptive information from the upper body (above T6, excepting the face and ear - the information from the face and ear is carried by the primary sensory trigeminal nucleus) to the contralateral thalamus via the medial lemniscus.

Inputs

It receives direct input from the mechanoreceptors of the upper body as well as indirect input from them via the spinal cord. It is also subject to descending control from the central nervous system.

Pathology

See also

- Fasciculus cuneatus

Additional images

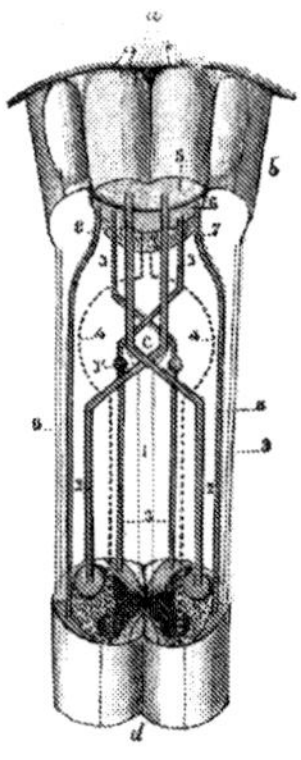
Decussation of pyramids.

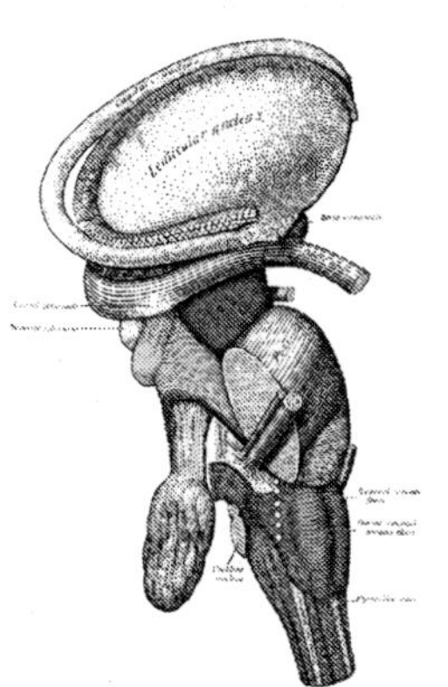
Dissection of brain-stem. Lateral view.

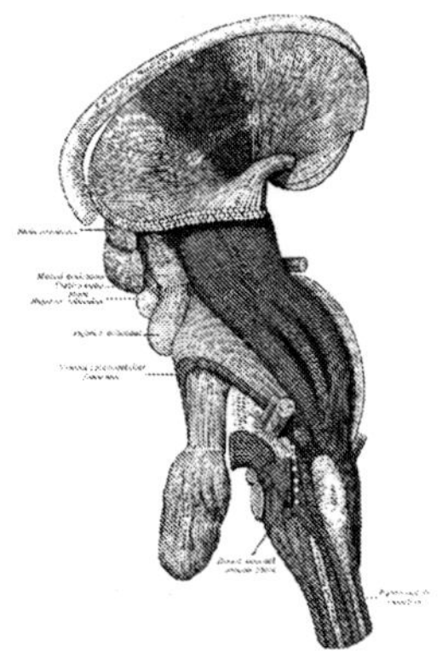
Deep dissection of brain-stem. Lateral view.

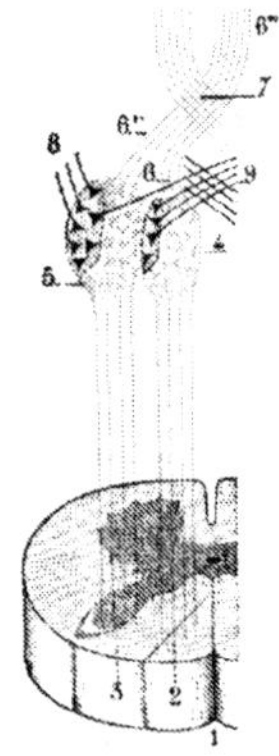
Superior terminations of the posterior fasciculi of the medulla spinalis.

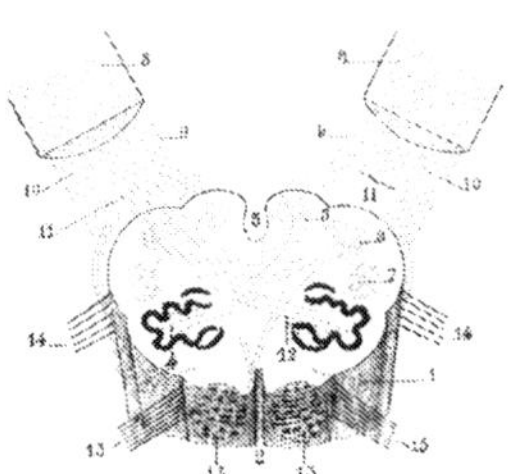
Diagram showing the course of the arcuate fibers.

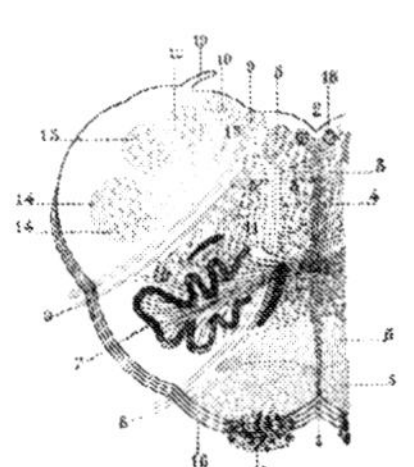
The formatio reticularis of the medulla oblongata, shown by a transverse section passing through the middle of the olive.

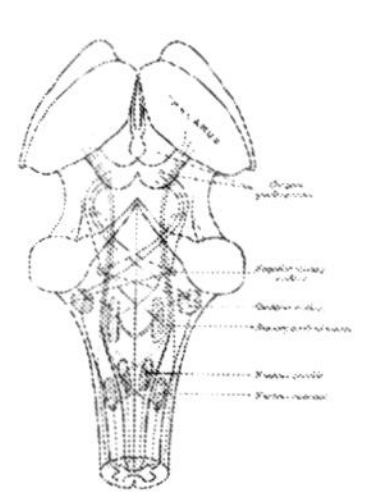
Scheme showing the course of the fibers of the lemniscus; medial lemniscus in blue, lateral in red.

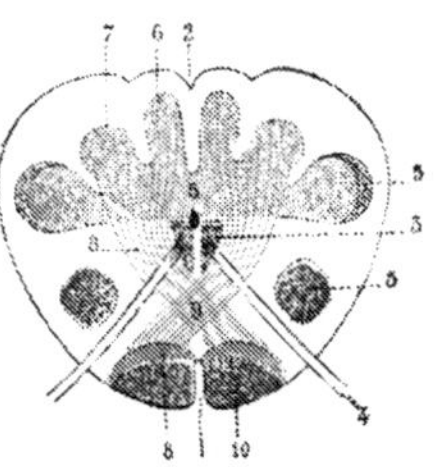
Transverse section passing through the sensory decussation.

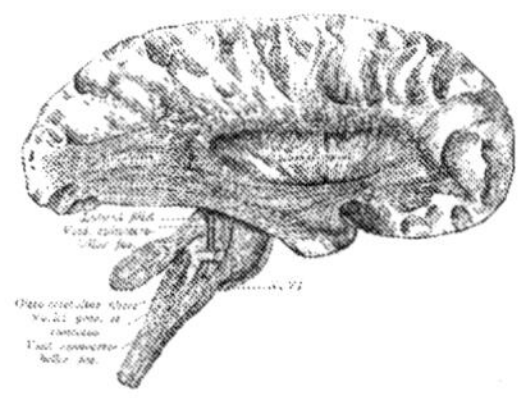
Deep dissection of cortex and brain-stem.

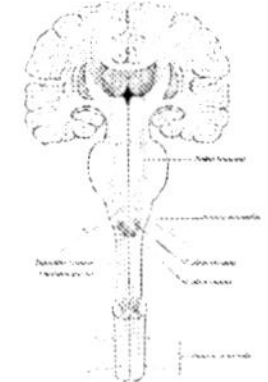
The sensory tract.

External links

- Brainstem at UWisc *04NGNC* [4]
- BrainMaps at UCDavis *Cuneate nucleus* [4]
- NIF Search - Cuneate Nucleus [5] via the Neuroscience Information Framework

Superior colliculus

Superior colliculus

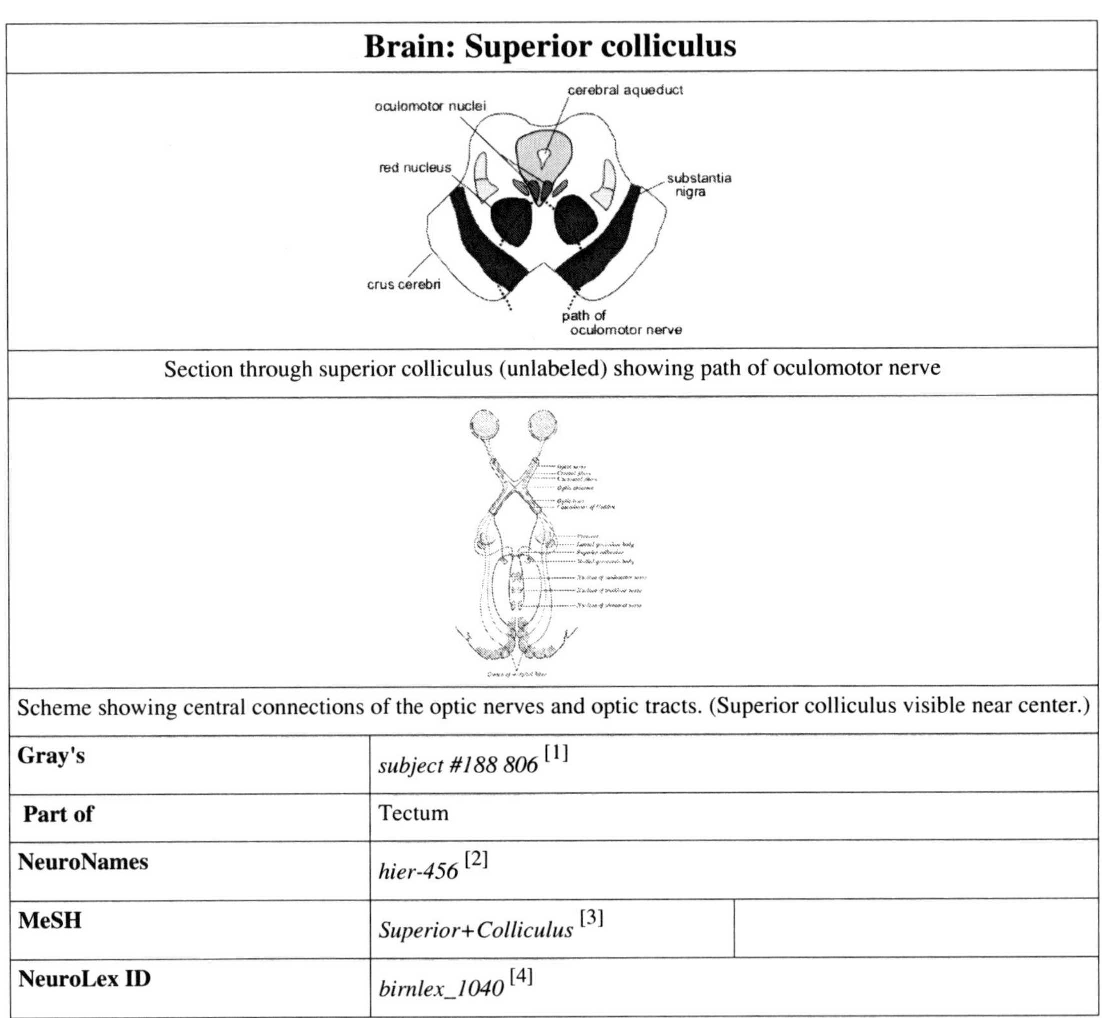

Section through superior colliculus (unlabeled) showing path of oculomotor nerve

Scheme showing central connections of the optic nerves and optic tracts. (Superior colliculus visible near center.)

Gray's	*subject #188 806* [1]	
Part of	Tectum	
NeuroNames	*hier-456* [2]	
MeSH	*Superior+Colliculus* [3]	
NeuroLex ID	*birnlex_1040* [4]	

The **optic tectum** or simply **tectum** is a paired structure that forms a major component of the vertebrate midbrain. In mammals this structure is more commonly called the **superior colliculus** (Latin, *higher hill*), but, even in mammals, the adjective *tectal* is commonly used. The tectum is a layered structure, with a number of layers that vary by species. The superficial layers are sensory-related, and receive input from the eyes as well as other sensory systems. The deep layers are motor-related, capable of activating eye movements as well as other responses. There are also intermediate layers, with multi-sensory cells and motor properties.

The general function of the tectal system is to direct behavioral responses toward specific points in egocentric ("body-centered") space. Each layer of the tectum contains a topographic map of the surrounding world in retinotopic coordinates, and activation of neurons at a particular point in the map evokes a response directed toward the corresponding point in space. In primates, the tectum ("superior colliculus") has been studied mainly with respect to its role in directing eye movements. Visual input from the retina, or "command" input from the cerebral cortex, create a "bump" of activity in the tectal map, which, if strong enough, induces a saccadic eye movement. Even in primates, however, the tectum is also involved in generating spatially directed head turns, arm-reaching movements, and shifts in attention that do not involve any overt movements. In other species, the tectum is involved in a wide range of responses, including whole-body turns in walking rats, swimming fishes, or flying birds; tongue-strikes toward prey in frogs; fang-strikes in snakes; etc.

In some non-mammal species, including fish and birds, the tectum is one of the largest components of the brain. In mammals, and especially primates, the massive expansion of the cerebral cortex reduces the tectum ("superior colliculus") to a much smaller fraction of the whole brain. Even there, however, it remains very important in terms of function as the primary integrating center for eye movements.

Note on terminology: the use by the literature of different terms for mammals and non-mammals, for what is really the same structure, creates problems for an article that attempts to encompass the full range of vertebrate species. There does not seem to be any way to handle this without causing either confusion or annoyance to some readers. The approach taken in this article is to follow the literature by using the term "superior colliculus" when discussing mammals, and "optic tectum" when discussing either specific non-mammalian species or vertebrates in general.

Evolution and comparative anatomy

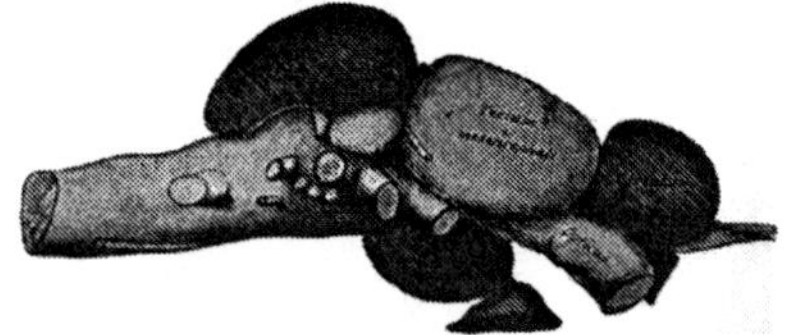
The brain of a cod, with the optic tectum highlighted

The optic tectum is one of the fundamental components of the vertebrate brain, existing across the full range of species from hagfish to human. (See the brain article for background.) Some aspects of the structure are very consistent, including a structure composed of a number of layers, with a dense input from the optic nerve to the superficial layers and another strong input conveying somatosensory input to deeper layers. Other aspects are highly variable, such as the total number of layers (from 3 in the African lungfish to 15 in the goldfish), and the number of different types of cells (from 2 in the lungfish to 27 in the house sparrow). In hagfish, lamprey, and shark it is a relatively small structure, but in teleost fish it is greatly expanded, in some cases becoming the largest structure in the brain. (See the adjoining drawing of a codfish brain.) In amphibians, reptiles, and especially birds it is also a very significant component, but in mammals it is dwarfed by the massive expansion of the cerebral cortex.

Lamprey

The lamprey has been extensively studied because it has a relatively simple brain that is thought in many respects to reflect the brain structure of early vertebrate ancestors. Beginning in the 1970s, Sten Grillner and his colleagues at the Karolinska Institut in Stockholm have used the lamprey as a model system to work out the fundamental principles of motor control in vertebrates, starting in the spinal cord and working upward into the brain. In a series of studies, they found that neural circuits within the spinal cord are capable of generating the rhythmic motor patterns that underlie swimming, that these circuits are controlled by specific locomotor areas in the brainstem and midbrain, and that these areas in turn are controlled by higher brain structures including the basal ganglia and tectum. In a study of the lamprey tectum published in 2007, they found that electrical stimulation could elicit eye movements, lateral bending movements, or swimming activity, and that the type, amplitude, and direction of movement varied as a function of the location within the tectum that was stimulated. These findings were interpreted as consistent with the idea that the tectum generates goal-directed locomotion in the lamprey as it does in other species.

Bats

Bats are not, in fact, blind, but they depend much more on echolocation than vision for navigation and prey capture. They obtain information about the surrounding world by emitting sonar chirps and then listening for the echoes. Their brains are highly specialized for this process, and some of these specializations appear in the superior colliculus. In bats, the retinal projection occupies only a thin zone just beneath the surface, but there are extensive inputs from auditory areas, and outputs to motor areas capable of orienting the ears, head, or body. Echoes coming from different directions activate neurons at different locations in the collicular layers, and activation of collicular neurons influences the chirps that the bats emit. Thus, there is a strong case that the superior colliculus performs the same sorts of functions for the auditory-guided behaviors of bats that it performs for the visual-guided behaviors of other species.

Bats are usually classified into two main groups: Microchiroptera (the most numerous, and commonly found throughout the world), and Megachiroptera (fruit bats, found in Asia, Africa and Australasia). With one exception, Megabats do not echolocate, and rely on a developed sense of vision to navigate. The visual receptive fields of neurons in the superior colliculus in these animals form a precise map of the retina, similar to that found in mammals such as cats and primates.

Structure and relations

The two superior colliculi sit below the thalamus and surround the pineal gland in the mesencephalon of vertebrate brains. It comprises the caudal aspect of the midbrain, posterior to the periaqueductal gray and immediately superior to the inferior colliculus. The inferior and superior colliculi are known collectively as the corpora quadrigemina (Latin, *quadruplet bodies*).

Neural circuit

The microstructure of the optic tectum / superior colliculus varies across species. As a general rule, there is always a clear distinction between superficial layers, which receive input primarily from the visual system and show primarily visual responses, and deeper layers, which receive many types of input and project to numerous motor-related brain areas. The distinction between these two zones is so clear and consistent that some anatomists have suggested that they should be considered separate brain structures.

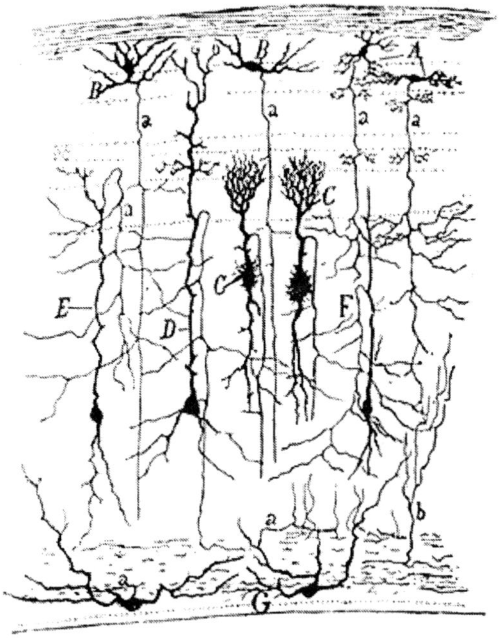

In mammals, neuroanatomists conventionally identify seven layers The top three layers are called *superficial*:

- **Lamina I** or **SZ**, the *stratum zonale*, is a thin layer consisting of small myelinated axons together with marginal and horizontal cells.
- **Lamina II** or **SGS**, the *stratum griseum superficiale* ("superficial gray"), contains many neurons of various shapes and sizes.
- **Lamina III** or **SO**, the *stratum opticum* ("optic layer"), consists mainly of axons coming from the optic nerve.

Drawing by Ramon y Cajal of several types of Golgi-stained neurons in the optic tectum of a sparrow.

Next come two *intermediate layers*:

- **Lamina IV** or **SGI**, the *stratum griseum intermediale* ("intermediate gray"), is the thickest layer, and is filled with many neurons of many sizes. This layer is often as thick as all the other layers together. It is often subdivided into "upper" and "lower" parts.

- **Lamina V** or **SAI**, the *stratum album intermediale* ("intermediate white"), consists mainly of fibers from various sources.

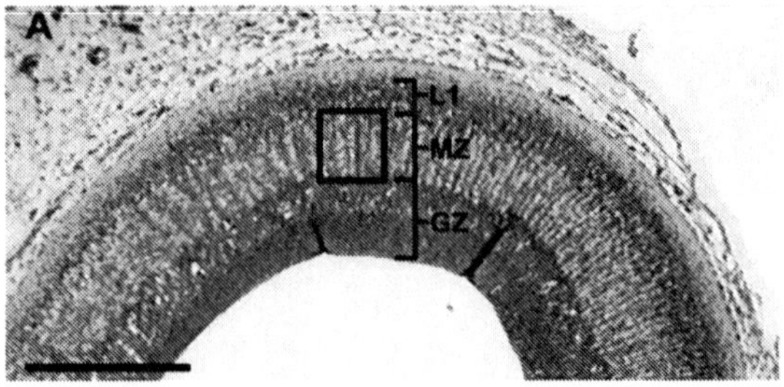

Finally come the two *deep layers*:

- **Lamina VI** or **SGP**, the *stratum griseum profundum* ("deep gray"), consists of loosely packed neurons and myelinated fibers.
- **Lamina VII** or **SAP**, the *stratum album profundum* ("deep white"), lying directly above the periaqueductal gray, consists entirely of fibers.

H&E stain of chicken optic tectum at E7 showing the generative zone (GZ), the migrating zone (MZ) and the first neuronal lamina (L1). Scale bar 200 μm. From Caltharp et al., 2007.

The superficial layers receive input mainly from the retina, vision-related areas of the cerebral cortex, and two tectal-related structures called the pretectum and *parabigeminal nucleus*. The retinal input encompasses the entire superficial zone, and is bilateral, although the contralateral portion is more extensive. The cortical input comes most heavily from the primary visual cortex (area 17), the secondary visual cortex (areas 18 and 19), and the frontal eye fields. The parabigeminal nucleus plays a very important role in tectal function that will be described below.

In addition to their distinctive inputs, the superficial and deep zones of the superior colliculus also have distinctive outputs. One of the most important outputs goes to the pulvinar and lateral intermediate areas of the thalamus, which in turn project to areas of the cerebral cortex that are involved in controlling eye movements. There are also projections from the superficial zone to the pretectal nuclei, lateral geniculate nucleus of the thalamus, and the parabigeminal nucleus. The projections from the deeper layers are more extensive. There are two large descending pathways, traveling to the brainstem and spinal cord, and numerous ascending projections to a variety of sensory and motor centers, including several that are involved in generating eye movements.

Mosaic structure

On detailed examination the collicular layers are actually not smooth sheets, but divided into a honeycomb arrangement of discrete columns. The clearest indication of columnar structure comes from the cholinergic inputs arising from the parabigeminal nucleus, whose terminals form evenly spaced clusters that extend from top to bottom of the tectum. Several other neurochemical markers including calretinin, parvalbumin, GAP-43, and NMDA receptors, and connections with numerous other brain structures in the brainstem and diencephalon, also show a corresponding inhomogeneity. The total number of columns has been estimated at around 100. The functional significance of this columnar architecture is not clear, but it is interesting that recent evidence has implicated the cholinergic inputs as part of a recurrent circuit producing winner-take-all dynamics within the tectum, as described in more detail below.

All species that have been examined — including mammals and non-mammals — show compartmentalization, but there are some systematic differences in the details of the arrangement. In species with a streak-type retina (mainly species with laterally placed eyes, such as rabbits and deer), the compartments cover the full extent of the SC. In species with a centrally placed fovea, however, the compartmentalization breaks down in the front (rostral) part of the SC. This portion of the SC contains many "fixation" neurons that fire continually while the eyes remain fixed in a constant position.

Nucleus Isthmii/Parabigeminalis

The optic tectum is closely associated with an adjoining structure called *nucleus isthmii*, which has drawn great interest recently because of new evidence that it makes a very important contribution to tectal function. In mammals, where the term *superior colliculus* is generally used instead of *optic tectum*, this area is called the *parabigeminal nucleus*. Once again, this is simply a case of two different names being used for the same structure. The nucleus isthmii is divided into two parts, called *pars magnocellularis* (**Imc**; "the part with the large cells") and *pars parvocellularis* (**Ipc**; "the part with the small cells"). *Imc* is also sometimes called *pars semilunaris*, because it is shaped like a half-moon, or rather crescent-moon, in cross-section.

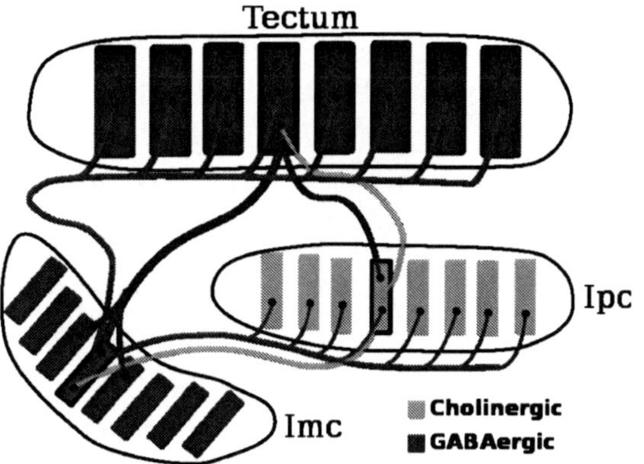

Schematic circuit diagram of topographic connections between the optic tectum and the two parts of nucleus isthmii.

As illustrated in the adjoining diagram, connections between the three areas — tectum, Ipc, and Imc — are topographic. Neurons in the superficial layers of the tectum project to corresponding points in Ipc and Imc. The projections to Ipc are tightly focused, while the projections to Imc are somewhat more diffuse. Ipc gives rise to tightly focused cholinergic projections both to Imc and the tectum. In the tectum, the cholinergic inputs from Ipc ramify to give rise to terminals that extend across an entire column, from top to bottom. Imc, in contrast, gives rise to GABAergic projections to Ipc and tectum that spread very broadly in the lateral dimensions, encompassing most of the retinotopic map. Thus, the tectum-Ipc-Imc circuit causes tectal activity to produce recurrent feedback that involves tightly focused excitation of a small column of neighboring tectal neurons, together with global inhibition of distant tectal neurons.

Function

The history of investigation of the optic tectum has been marked by several large shifts in opinion. Before about 1970, most studies involved non-mammals — fish, frogs, birds - that is, species in which the tectum is the dominant structure that receives input from the eyes. The general view then was that the tectum, in these species, is the main visual center in the non-mammalian brain, and, as a consequence, is involved in a wide variety of behaviors. From the 1970s to 1990s, however, neural recordings from mammals, mostly monkeys, focused primarily on the role of the superior colliculus in controlling eye movements. This line of investigation came to dominate the literature to such a degree that the majority opinion was that eye-movement control is the only important function in mammals, a view still reflected in many current textbooks. In the late 1990s, however, experiments using animals whose heads were free to move showed clearly that the SC actually produces *gaze shifts*, usually composed of combined head and eye movements, rather than eye movements *per se*. This discovery reawakened interest in the full breadth of functions of the superior colliculus, and led to studies of multisensory integration in a variety of species and situations. Nevertheless, the role of the SC in controlling eye movements is understood in much greater depth than any other function.

Behavioral studies have shown that the SC is not needed for object recognition, but plays a critical role in the ability to direct behaviors toward specific objects, and can support this ability even in the absence of the cerebral cortex. Thus, cats with major damage to the visual cortex cannot recognize objects, but may still be able to follow and orient toward moving stimuli, although more slowly than usual. If one half of the SC is removed, however, the cats will circle constantly toward the side of the lesion, and orient compulsively toward objects located there, but fail to orient at all toward objects located in the opposite hemifield. These deficits diminish over time but never disappear.

Eye movements

In primates, eye movements can be divided into several types: *fixation*, in which the eyes are directed toward a motionless object, with eye movements only to compensate for movements of the head; *smooth pursuit*, in which the eyes move steadily to track a moving object; *saccades*, in which the eyes move very rapidly from one location to another; and *vergence*, in which the eyes move simultaneously in opposite directions to obtain or maintain single binocular vision. The superior colliculus is involved in all of these, but its role in saccades has been studied most intensively.

Each of the two colliculi — one on each side of the brain — contains a two-dimensional map representing half of the visual field. The fovea — the region of maximum sensitivity — is represented at the front edge of the map, and the periphery at the back edge. Eye movements are evoked by activity in the deep layers of the SC. During fixation, neurons near the front edge — the foveal zone — are tonically active. During smooth pursuit, neurons a small distance from the front edge are activated, leading to small eye movements. For saccades, neurons are activated in a region that represents the point to which the saccade will be directed. Just prior to a saccade, activity rapidly builds up at the target location and decreases in other parts of the SC. The coding is rather broad, so that for any given saccade the activity profile forms a "hill" that encompasses a substantial fraction of the collicular map: The location of the peak of this "hill" represents the saccade target.

The SC encodes the target of a gaze shift, but it does not seem to specify the precise movements needed to get there. The decomposition of a gaze shift into head and eye movements and the precise trajectory of the eye during a saccade depend on integration of collicular and non-collicular signals by downstream motor areas, in ways that are not yet well understood. Regardless of how the movement is evoked or performed, the SC encodes it in "retinotopic" coordinates: that is, a given SC activation pattern specifies a given offset from the current gaze direction, irrespective of the initial position of the eyes.

There has been some controversy about whether the SC merely commands eye movements, and leaves the execution to other structures, or whether it actively participates in the performance of a saccade. In 1991, Munoz et al., on the basis of data they collected, argued that, during a saccade, the "hill" of activity in the SC moves gradually, to reflect the changing offset of the eye from the target location while the saccade is progressing. At present, however, the predominant view is that, although the "hill" does shift slightly during a saccade, it does not shift in the steady and proportionate way that the "moving hill" hypothesis predicts.

The output from the motor sector of the SC goes to a set of midbrain and brainstem nuclei, which transform the "place" code used by the SC into the "rate" code used by oculomotor neurons. Eye movements are generated by six muscles, arranged in three orthogonally-aligned pairs. Thus, at the level of the final common path, eye movements are encoded in essentially a Cartesian coordinate system.

Although the SC receives a strong input directly from the retina, in primates it is largely under the control of the cerebral cortex, which contains several areas that are involved in determining eye movements. The frontal eye fields, a portion of the motor cortex, are involved in triggering intentional saccades, and an adjoining area, the supplementary eye fields, are involved in organizing groups of saccades into sequences. The parietal eye fields, farther back in the brain, are involved mainly in reflexive saccades, made in response to changes in the view.

The SC only receives visual inputs in its superficial layers, whereas the deeper layers of the colliculus receive also auditory and somatosensory inputs and are connected to many sensorimotor areas of the brain. The colliculus as a whole is thought to help orient the head and eyes toward something seen and heard.

The superior colliculus also receives auditory information from the inferior colliculus. This auditory information is integrated with the visual information already present to produce the ventriloquist effect.

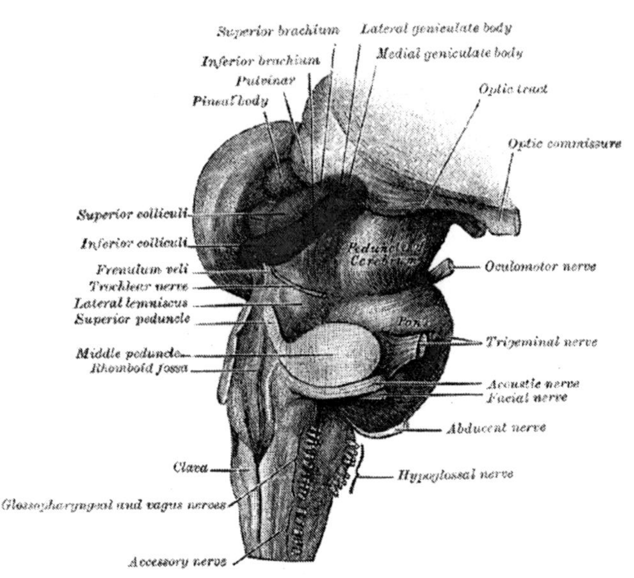

Hind- and mid-brains; postero-lateral view. Superior colliculus labeled in blue.

Diversity

Primates

It is usually accepted that the primate superior colliculus is unique among mammals, in that it does not contain a complete map of the visual field seen by the contralateral eye. Instead, like the visual cortex and lateral geniculate nucleus, each colliculus represents only the contralateral half of the visual field, up to the midline, and excludes a representation of the ipsilateral half. This functional characteristic is explained by the absence, in primates, of anatomical connections between the retinal ganglion cells in the temporal half of the retina and the contralateral superior colliculus. In other mammals, the retinal ganglion cells throughout the contralateral retina project to the contralateral colliculus. This distinction between primates and non-primates has been one of the key lines of evidence in support of the flying primates theory proposed by Australian neuroscientist Jack Pettigrew in 1986, after he discovered that flying foxes (megabats) resemble primates in terms of the pattern of anatomical connections between the retina and superior colliculus.

Other vertebrates

In snakes that can detect infrared radiation, such as pythons and pit vipers, the initial neural input is through the trigeminal nerve instead of the optic nerve. The rest of the processing is similar to that of the visual sense and, thus, involves the optic tectum.

See also

- inferior colliculus
- Lateral geniculate nucleus
- List of regions in the human brain

Additional images

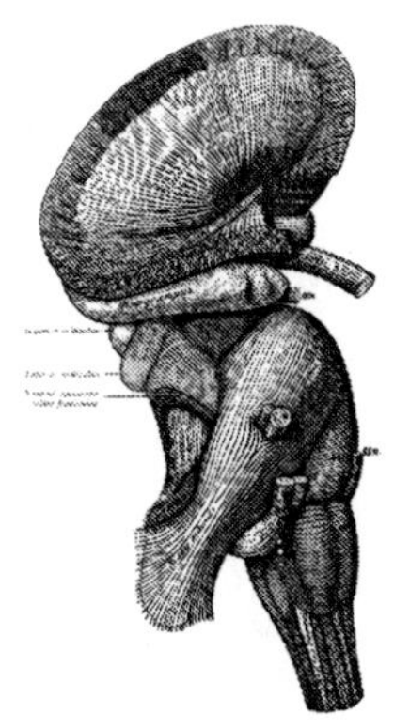
Superficial dissection of brain-stem. Lateral view.

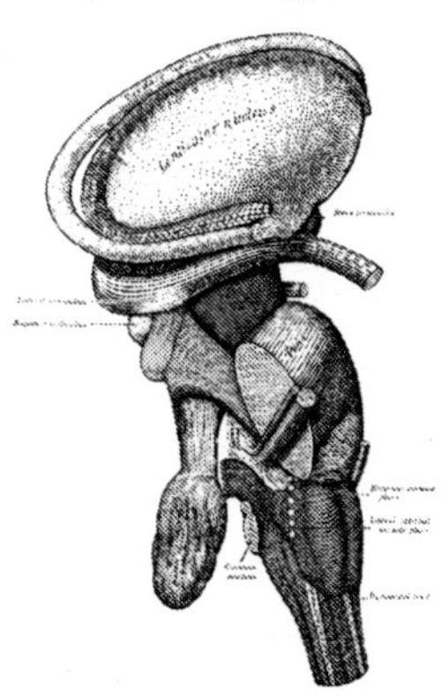
Dissection of brain-stem. Lateral view.

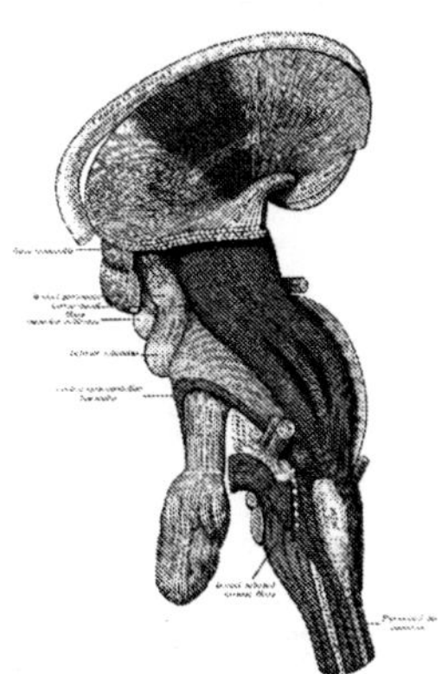
Deep dissection of brain-stem. Lateral view.

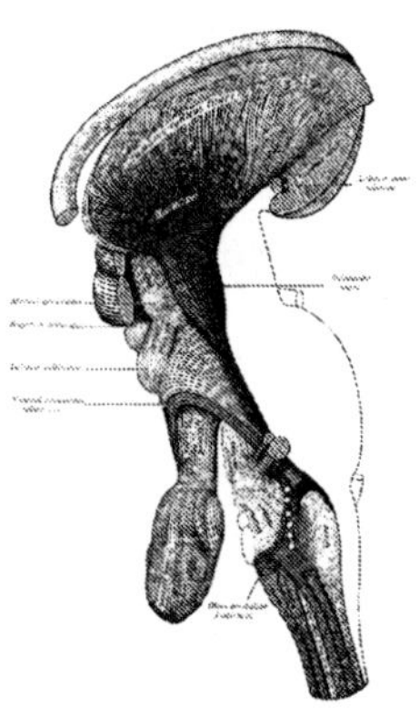
Deep dissection of brain-stem. Lateral view.

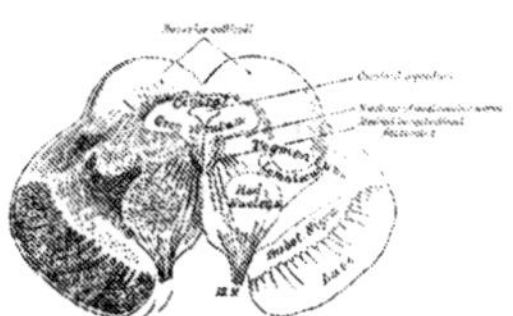
Transverse section of mid-brain at level of superior colliculi.

External links

- Brainstem at UWisc *23Colliculus* [5]
- BrainMaps at UCDavis *superior colliculus* [6]

References

- Chevalier, G; Mana S (2000). "Honeycomb-like structure of the intermediate layers of the rat superior colliculus, with additional observations in several other mammals: AChE patterning". *J Comp Neurol* **419** (2): 137–53. doi:10.1002/(SICI)1096-9861(20000403)419:2<137::AID-CNE1>3.0.CO;2-6 [7]. PMID 10722995 [8].
- Dean, P; Redgrave P, Westby GW (1989). "Event or emergency? Two response systems in the mammalian superior colliculus". *Trends Neurosci* **12** (4): 137–47.

doi:10.1016/0166-2236(89)90052-0 [9]. PMID 2470171 [10].

- Grillner, S (2003). "The motor infrastructure: from ion channels to neuronal networks". *Nat Rev Neurosci* **4** (7): 573–86. doi:10.1038/nrn1137 [11]. PMID 12838332 [12].
- Hartline, PH; Kass L, Loop MS (1978). "Merging of modalities in the optic tectum: infrared and visual integration in rattlesnakes". *Science* **199** (4334): 1225–9. doi:10.1126/science.628839 [13]. PMID 628839 [14].
- Huerta, MF; Harting JK (1984). Vanegas H. ed. *Comparative Neurology of the Optic Tectum*. New York: Plenum Press. pp. 687–773. ISBN 9780306412363.
- Illing, R-B (1996). "The mosaic architecture of the superior colliculus". *Prog Brain Res* **112**: 17–34. doi:10.1016/S0079-6123(08)63318-X [15]. PMID 8979818 [16].
- King, AJ; Schnupp JWH, Carlile S, Smith AL, Thompson ID (1996). "The development of topographically-aligned maps of visual an auditory space in the superior colliculus". *Prog Brain Res* **112**: 335–350. doi:10.1016/S0079-6123(08)63340-3 [17]. PMID 8979840 [18].
- Klier, EM; Wang H, Crawford JD (2001). "The superior colliculus encodes gaze commands in retinal coordinates" [19] (PDF). *Nat Neurosci* **4** (6): 627–32. doi:10.1038/88450 [20]. PMID 11369944 [21].
- Klier, E; Wang H, Crawford D (2003). "Three-dimensional eye-head coordination is implemented downstream from the superior colliculus" [22]. *J Neurophysiol* **89** (5): 2839–53. doi:10.1152/jn.00763.2002 [23]. PMID 12740415 [24].
- Krauzlis, R; Liston D, Carello C (2004). "Target selection and the superior colliculus: goals, choices and hypotheses". *Vision Res* **44** (12): 1445–51. doi:10.1016/j.visres.2004.01.005 [25]. PMID 15066403 [26].
- Kustov, A; Robinson D (1996). "Shared neural control of attentional shifts and eye movements". *Nature* **384** (6604): 74–77. doi:10.1038/384074a0 [27]. PMID 8900281 [28].
- Lane, RH; Allman JM, Kaas JH, Miezin FM (1973). "The visuotopic organization of the superior colliculus of the owl monkey (*Aotus trivirgatus*) and the bush baby (*Galago senegalensis*)". *Brain Res* **60** (2): 335–49. doi:10.1016/0006-8993(73)90794-4 [29]. PMID 4202853 [30].
- Lunenburger, L; Kleiser R, Stuphorn V, Miller LE, Hoffmann KP (2001). "A possible role of the superior colliculus in eye–hand coordination". *Prog Brain Res* **134**: 109–25. doi:10.1016/S0079-6123(01)34009-8 [31]. PMID 11702538 [32].
- Mana, S; Chevalier G (2001). "Honeycomb-like structure of the intermediate layers of the rat superior colliculus: afferent and efferent connections". *Neuroscience* **103** (3): 673–93. doi:10.1016/S0306-4522(01)00026-4 [33]. PMID 11274787 [34].
- Maximino, C; Soares, Daphne (2008). "Evolutionary changes in the complexity of the tectum of nontetrapods: a cladistic approach" [35]. *PLOS One* **3** (10): e385. doi:10.1371/journal.pone.0003582

[36]. PMID 18974789 [37]. PMC 2571994 [38].

- Munoz, DP; Pélisson D, Guitton D (1991). "Movement of activity on the superior colliculus motor map during gaze shifts" [39] (PDF). *Science* **251** (4999): 1358–60. doi:10.1126/science.2003221 [40]. PMID 2003221 [41].
- Northcutt, RG (2002). "Understanding vertebrate brain evolution" [42]. *Integr Comp Biol* **42**: 743–6. doi:10.1093/icb/42.4.743 [43].
- Pettigrew, JD (1986). "Flying primates? Megabats have the advanced pathway from eye to midbrain". *Science* **231** (4743): 1304–6. doi:10.1126/science.3945827 [44]. PMID 3945827 [45].
- Pierrot-Deseilligny, C; Müri RM, Ploner CJ, Gaymard B, Rivaud-Péchoux S (2003). "Cortical control of ocular saccades in humans: a model for motricity". *Prog Brain Res* **142**: 3–17. doi:10.1016/S0079-6123(03)42003-7 [46]. PMID 12693251 [47].
- Saitoh, K; Ménard A, Grillner S (2007). "Tectal control of locomotion, steering, and eye movements in lamprey" [48]. *J Neurophysiol* **97** (4): 3093–108. doi:10.1152/jn.00639.2006 [49]. PMID 17303814 [50].
- Soetedjo, R; Kaneko CR, Fuchs AF (2002). "Evidence against a moving hill in the superior colliculus during saccadic eye movements in the monkey" [51]. *J Neurophysiol* **87** (6): 2778–89. PMID 12037180 [52].
- Sparks, DL (1999). "Conceptual issues related to the role of the superior colliculus in the control of gaze". *Curr Op Neurobiol* **6** (6): 698–707. PMID 10607648 [53].
- Sparks, DL; Gandhi NJ (2003). "Single-cell signals: an oculomotor perspective". *Prog Brain Res* **142**: 35–53. doi:10.1016/S0079-6123(03)42005-0 [54]. PMID 12693253 [55].
- Sprague, JM (1996). "Neural mechanisms of visual orienting responses". *Prog Brain Res* **112**: 1–15. doi:10.1016/S0079-6123(08)63317-8 [56]. PMID 8979817 [57].
- Stein, BE; Clamman HP (1981). "Control of pinna movements and sensorimotor register in cat superior colliculus". *Brain Behav Evol* **19** (3-4): 180–192. doi:10.1159/000121641 [58]. PMID 7326575 [59].
- Ulanovsky, N; Moss CF (2008). "What the bat's voice tells the bat's brain" [60]. *PNAS* **105** (25): 8491–98. doi:10.1073/pnas.0703550105 [61]. PMID 18562301 [62].
- Valentine, D; Moss CF (1997). "Spatially selective auditory responses in the superior colliculus of the echolocating bat" [63]. *J Neurosci* **17** (5): 1720–33. PMID 9030631 [64].
- Wallace, MT; Meredith MA, Stein BE (1998). "Multisensory integration in the superior colliculus of the alert cat" [65]. *J Neurophysiol* **80** (2): 1006–10. PMID 9705489 [66].

Inferior colliculus

Inferior colliculus

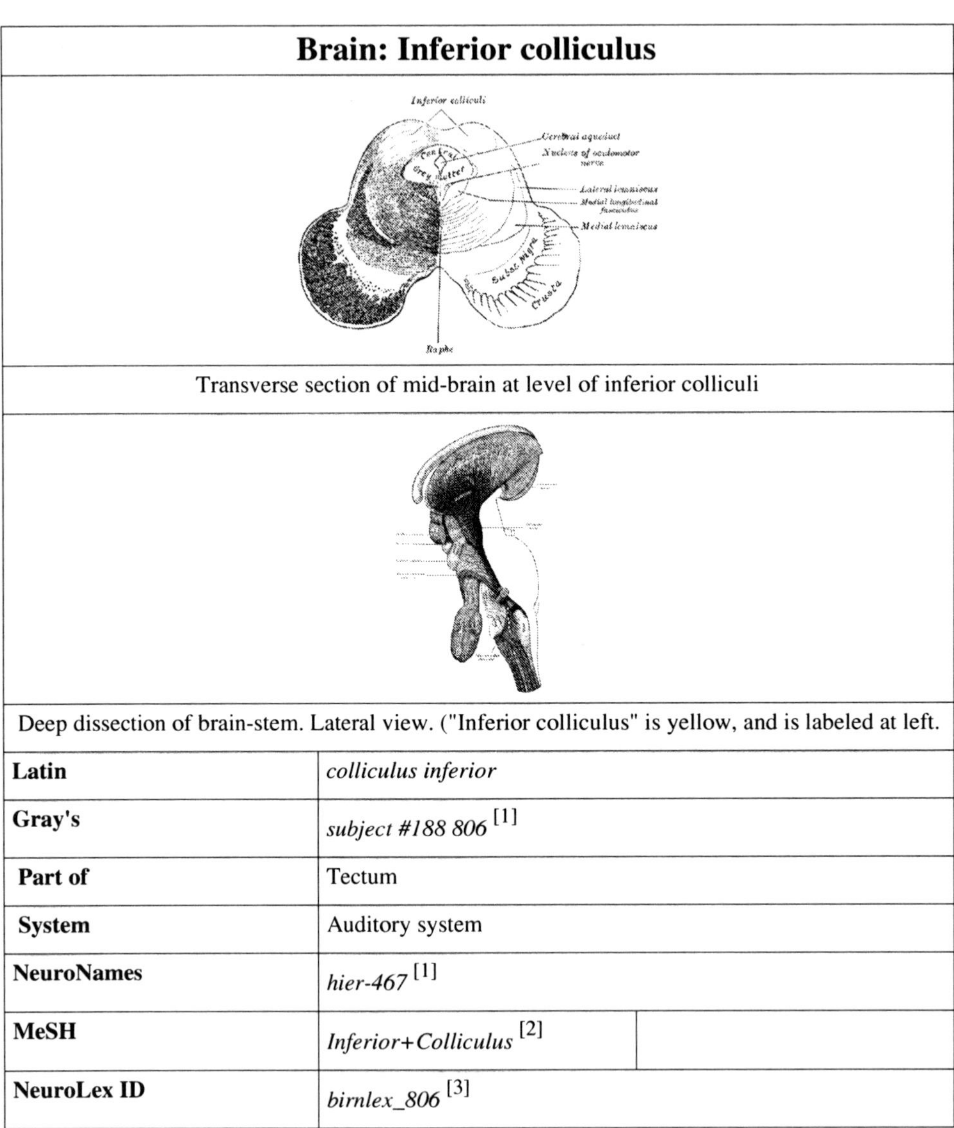

Brain: Inferior colliculus	
Transverse section of mid-brain at level of inferior colliculi	
Deep dissection of brain-stem. Lateral view. ("Inferior colliculus" is yellow, and is labeled at left.	
Latin	*colliculus inferior*
Gray's	*subject #188 806* [1]
Part of	Tectum
System	Auditory system
NeuroNames	*hier-467* [1]
MeSH	*Inferior+Colliculus* [2]
NeuroLex ID	*birnlex_806* [3]

The **inferior colliculus** (IC) (Latin, *lower hill*) is the principal midbrain nucleus of the auditory pathway and receives input from several more peripheral brainstem nuclei in the auditory pathway, as well as inputs from the auditory cortex. The inferior colliculus has three subdivisions: the central nucleus (CIC), a dorsal cortex (DCIC) by which it is surrounded, and an external cortex (ICX) which is located laterally. Its bimodal neurons are implied in auditory-somatosensory interaction, receiving projections from somatosensory nuclei. This multisensory integration may underlie a filtering of self-effected sounds from vocalisation, chewing, or respiration activities.

The inferior colliculi together with the superior colliculi form the eminences of the corpora quadrigemina, and also part of the tectal region of the midbrain. The inferior colliculus lies caudal to its counterpart - the superior colliculus - above the trochlear nerve, and at the base of the projection of the medial geniculate nucleus (MGN) and the lateral geniculate nucleus (LGN).

Relationship to auditory system

The inferior colliculi of the midbrain are located just below the visual processing centers known as the superior colliculi. The inferior colliculus is the first place where vertically orienting data from the fusiform cells in the dorsal cochlear nucleus can finally synapse with horizontally orienting data. This homecoming of the aural dimensions puts these dual mesencephalic bumps in the position to fully integrate all the sound location data.

The inferior colliculus function as a master computer both in regard to its hardware (complex connections) and its software (internal organization). IC are large auditory nuclei on the right and left sides of the midbrain. It is divided into three parts, the Central Nucleus of IC (CNIC), dorsal cortex and lateral cortex; however, CNIC is the principal way station for ascending auditory information in the IC.

1. Input and Output Connection of IC The input connections to the inferior colliculus are composed of many brainstem nuclei. All nuclei except the contralateral ventral nucleus of the lateral lemniscus (LL) send projections to the central nucleus (CNIC) bilaterally. It has been shown that great majority of auditory fibers ascending in the lateral lemniscus terminate in the CNIC. In addition, the IC receives descending inputs from the auditory cortex, medial geniculate body (MGB), and superior colliculus (SC).

The inferior colliculus receives input from both the ipsilateral and contralateral cochlear nucleus and respectively the corresponding ears. Of course, there is some lateralization, the dorsal projections (containing vertical data) only project to the contralateral inferior colliculus. This inferior colliculus contralateral to the ear it is receiving the most information from, then projects to its ipsilateral medial geniculate nucleus.

The medial geniculate body (MGB) is the output connection from inferior colliculus and the last subcortical way station. The MGB is composed of ventral, dorsal, and medial divisions, which are relatively similar in humans and other mammals. The ventral division receives auditory signals from the central nucleus of the IC.

2. Function of IC

The majority of the ascending fibers from LL project to IC, which means major ascending auditory pathway converge here. IC appears as an integrative station and switchboard as well. It is involved in the integration and routing of multi-modal sensory perception, mainly the startle reflex and vestibulo-ocular reflex. It is also responsive to specific amplitude modulation frequencies and this might be responsible for detection of pitch. In addition, spatial localization by binaural hearing is a related function of IC as well.

The inferior colliculus has a relatively high metabolism in the brain. The Conrad Simon Memorial Research Initiative measured the blood flow of the IC and put a number at 1.80 cc/g/min in the cat brain. For reference, the runner up in the included measurements was the somatosensory cortex at 1.53. This indicates that the inferior colliculus is metabolically more active than many other parts of the brain. The hippocampus, normally considered to use up a disproportionate amount of energy, was not measured or compared.

Skottun *et al.* measured the interaural time difference sensitivity of single neurons in the inferior colliculus, and used these to predict behavioural performance. The predicted just noticeable difference was comparable to that achieved by humans in behavioral tests. This suggested that by the level of the inferior colliculus, integration of information over multiple neurons is unnecessary (see population code).

Abbreviations: CNIC: Central Nucleus of IC; AVCN: Anterior Ventral Cochlear Nucleus; PVCN: Posterior Ventral Cochlear Nucleus; SCN: Superior Colliculus Nucleus; LSO: Lateral Superior Olive; MSO: Medial Superior Olive; DNLL: Dorsal Nucleus of the Lateral Lemniscus; MGB: Medial Geniculate Body; SC: Superior Colliculus; TB: Trapezoid Body

See also

- Auditory system
- List of regions in the human brain

Additional images

Superficial dissection of brain-stem. Lateral view.

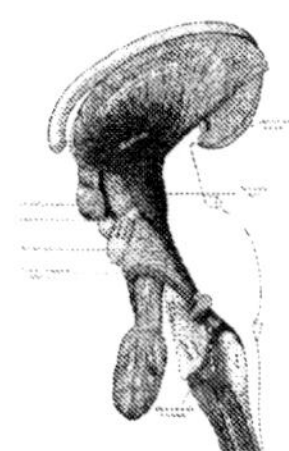
Deep dissection of brain-stem. Lateral view.

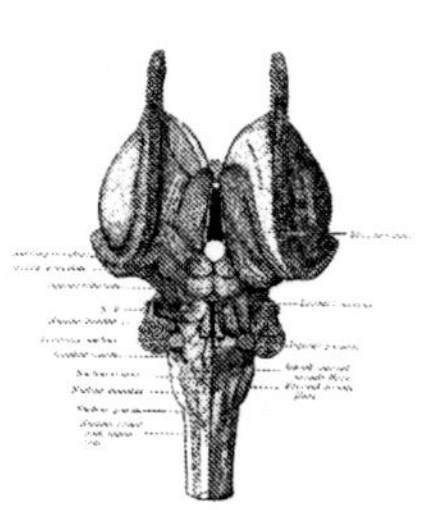
Dissection of brain-stem. Dorsal view.

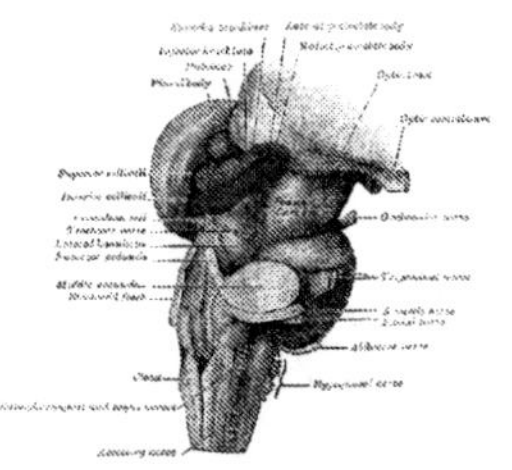
Hind- and mid-brains; postero-lateral view.

External links

- Brainstem at UWisc *23Colliculus* [5]
- BrainMaps at UCDavis *inferior colliculus* [4]

Midbrain tectum

Midbrain tectum

Brain: Midbrain tectum	
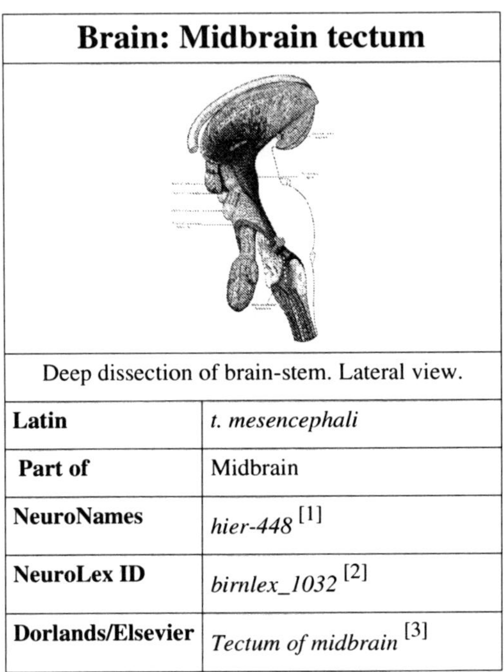	
Deep dissection of brain-stem. Lateral view.	
Latin	*t. mesencephali*
Part of	Midbrain
NeuroNames	*hier-448* [1]
NeuroLex ID	*birnlex_1032* [2]
Dorlands/Elsevier	*Tectum of midbrain* [3]

The **tectum** (Latin: *roof*) is a region of the brain, specifically the dorsal part of the mesencephalon (midbrain). This is contrasted with the tegmentum, which refers to the region ventral to the ventricular system. It is responsible for auditory and visual reflexes.

It is derived in embryonic development from the alar plate of the neural tube.

Colliculi

In adult humans it is present only in the mesencephalon as the inferior and the superior colliculi.

- The superior colliculus is involved in preliminary visual processing and control of eye movements. In non-mammalian vertebrates it serves as the main visual area of the brain, functionally analogous to the visual areas of the cerebral cortex in mammals.
- The inferior colliculus is involved in auditory processing. It receives input from various brain stem nuclei and projects to the medial geniculate nucleus of the thalamus, which relays auditory

information to the primary auditory cortex.

Both colliculi also have descending projections to the paramedian pontine reticular formation and spinal cord, and thus can be involved in responses to stimuli faster than cortical processing would allow. Collectively the colliculi are referred to as the corpora quadrigemina.

Related terms

The term "tectal plate" (or "quadrigeminal plate") is used to describe the junction of the gray and white matter in the embryo. (, NeuroNames *ancil-453* [4])

See also

- List of regions in the human brain
- Tectospinal tract

External links

- Diagram [5]
- Photo [6]
- Roche Lexicon - illustrated navigator, at Elsevier *13048.000-3* [7]

Periaqueductal gray

Periaqueductal gray

Brain: Periaqueductal gray

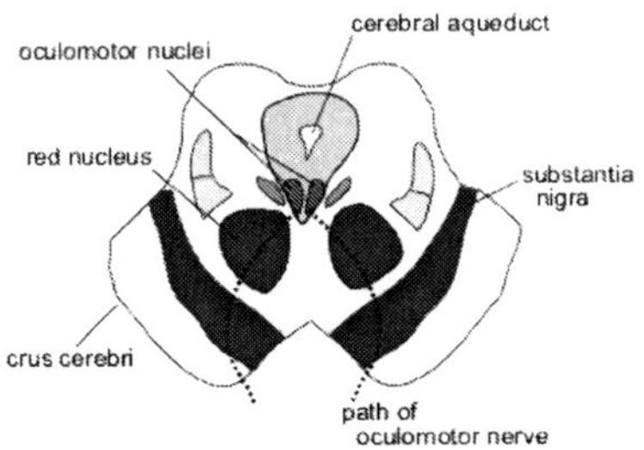

Section through superior colliculus showing path of oculomotor nerve. Periaqueductal gray is the gray area just peripheral to the cerebral aqueduct.)

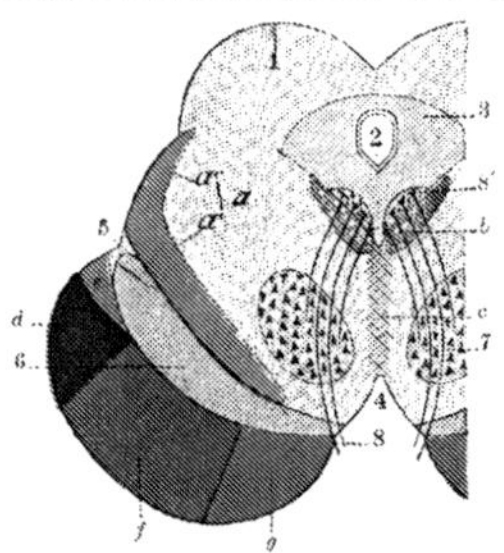

Coronal section through mid-brain.
1. Corpora quadrigemina.
2. Cerebral aqueduct.
3. Central gray stratum.
4. Interpeduncular space.
5. Sulcus lateralis.
6. Substantia nigra.
7. Red nucleus of tegmentum.
8. Oculomotor nerve, with 8', its nucleus of origin. a. Lemniscus (in blue) with a' the medial lemniscus and a" the lateral lemniscus. b. Medial longitudinal fasciculus. c. Raphé. d. Temporopontine fibers. e. Portion of medial lemniscus, which runs to the lentiform nucleus and insula. f. Cerebrospinal fibers. g. Frontopontine fibers.

Latin	*s. grisea centralis*
Gray's	*subject #188 806* [1]
NeuroNames	*hier-501* [1]

MeSH	*Periaqueductal+Gray* [2]	

Periaqueductal gray (PAG; also called the "central gray") is the gray matter located around the cerebral aqueduct within the tegmentum of the midbrain. It plays a role in the descending modulation of pain and in defensive behaviour. The ascending pain and temperature fibers of the spinothalamic tract also send information to the PAG via the spinomesencephalic tract (so-named because the fibers originate in the spine and terminate in the PAG, in the mesencephalon or midbrain).

Role in analgesia

Stimulation of the periaqueductal gray matter of the midbrain activates enkephalin-releasing neurons that project to the raphe nuclei in the brainstem. 5-HT (serotonin) released from the raphe nuclei descends to the dorsal horn of the spinal cord where it forms excitatory connections with the "inhibitory interneurons" located in Laminae II (aka the substantia gelatinosa). When activated, these interneurons release either enkephalin or dynorphin (endogenous opioid neurotransmitters), which bind to mu opioid receptors on the axons of incoming C and A-delta fibers carrying pain signals from nociceptors activated in the periphery. The activation of the mu-opioid receptor inhibits the release of substance P from these incoming first-order neurons and, in turn, inhibits the activation of the second-order neuron that is responsible for transmitting the pain signal up the spinothalamic tract to the ventroposteriolateral nucleus (VPL) of the thalamus. The nociceptive signal was inhibited before it was able to reach the cortical areas that interpret the signal as "pain" (such as the anterior cingulate). This is sometimes referred to as the Gate control theory of pain and is supported by the fact that electrical stimulation of the PAG results in immediate and profound analgesia.

Four known kinds of opioid receptors have been identified: mu, kappa, sigma and delta. Synthetic opioid and opioid-derivative drugs activate these receptors (possibly by acting on the PAG directly, where these receptors are densely expressed) to produce analgesia. These drugs include heroin, morphine, pethidine, hydrocodone, oxycodone, and similar pain-reducing compounds.

Role in defensive behavior

Stimulation of the dorsal and lateral aspects of the PAG (in the rat) can provoke defensive responses characterised by freezing immobility, running, jumping, tachycardia, and increases in blood pressure and muscle tonus. In contrast, stimulation of the caudal ventrolateral PAG can result in an immobile, relaxed posture known as quiescence, whereas its inhibition leads to increased locomotor activity.

Lesions of the caudal ventrolateral PAG can greatly reduce conditioned freezing, whereas lesions of the dorsal aspect can reduce innate defensive behavior, virtually "taming" the animal.

Role in reproductive behavior

Neurons of the PAG are excited by endorphins and by opiate analgesics. It also plays a role in female copulatory behavior (see Lordosis behavior) via a pathway from the ventromedial nucleus of the hypothalamus.

Role in consciousness

If there is a lesion in the PAG, then consciousness is lost. This observation does not mean that the PAG, itself, is the center of consciousness, but rather that it is a critically-needed part of it.

Additional images

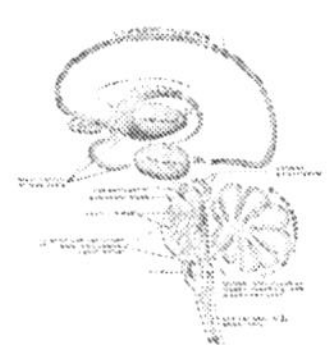

Schematic representation of the chief ganglionic categories (I to V).

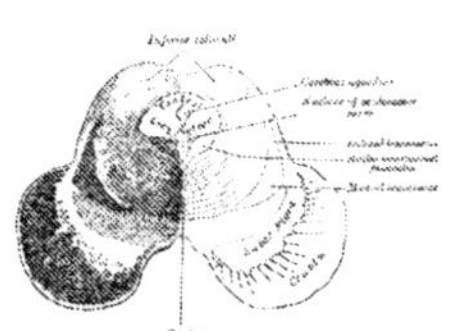

Transverse section of mid-brain at level of inferior colliculi.

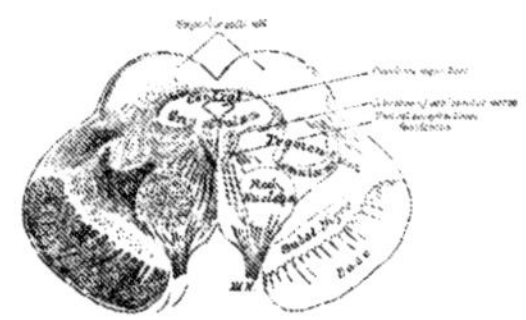

Transverse section of mid-brain at level of superior colliculi.

External links

- BrainMaps at UCDavis *Periaqueductal gray* [3]

Olivary body

Olivary body

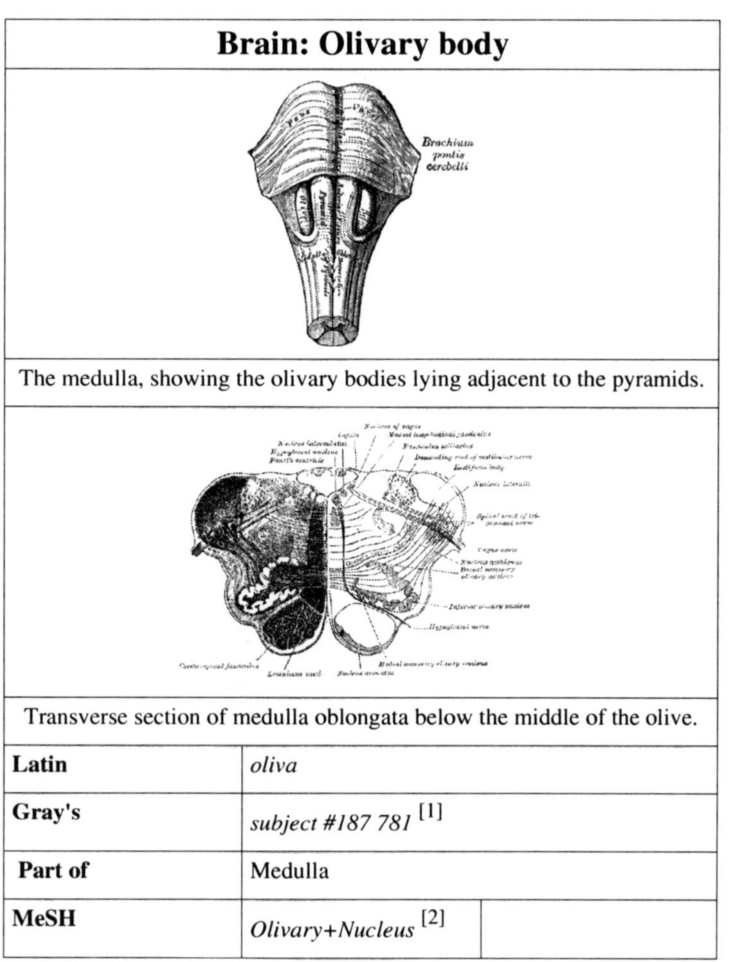

Brain: Olivary body		
The medulla, showing the olivary bodies lying adjacent to the pyramids.		
Transverse section of medulla oblongata below the middle of the olive.		
Latin	*oliva*	
Gray's	*subject #187 781* [1]	
Part of	Medulla	
MeSH	*Olivary+Nucleus* [2]	

In anatomy, the **olivary bodies** or simply **olives** (Latin *oliva* and *olivae*, singular and plural, respectively) are a pair of prominent oval structures in the medulla oblongata, the lower portion of the brainstem. They contain the **olivary nuclei**.

External anatomy

The olivary body is located on the anterior surface of the medulla lateral to the pyramid, from which it is separated by the antero-lateral sulcus and the fibers of the hypoglossal nerve.

Behind, it is separated from the postero-lateral sulcus by the ventral spinocerebellar fasciculus. In the depression between the upper end of the olive and the pons lies the vestibulocochlear nerve.

In humans, it measures about 1.25 cm. in length, and between its upper end and the pons there is a slight depression to which the roots of the facial nerve are attached.

The external arcuate fibers wind across the lower part of the pyramid and olive and enter the inferior peduncle.

Olivary nuclei

The olive consists of two separate parts:

- The inferior olivary nucleus or the inferior olivary complex,

which is a part of the olivo-cerebellar system and is mainly involved in cerebellar motor-learning and function.

- The superior olivary nucleus is considered part of the pons and is a part of the auditory system, aiding the perception of sound.

The inferior olive in itself is divided to 3 main nuclei:.

- The **primary olivary nucleus** (PO) which consist of the major laminar structure.
- The **medial accessory olivary nucleus** (MAO) lies between the primary olivary nucleus and the pyramid, and forms a curved lamina, the concavity of which is directed laterally.
- The **dorsal accessory olivary nucleus** (DAO) is the smallest, and appears on transverse section as a curved lamina behind the primary olivary nucleus.

small additional inferior olivary structures consist of the dorsal cap of Kooy and the ventrolateral outgrowth.

Additional images

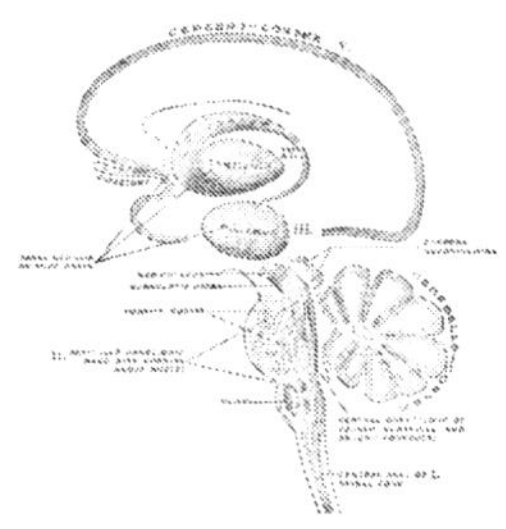
Schematic representation of the chief ganglionic categories (I to V).

Superficial dissection of brain-stem. Lateral view.

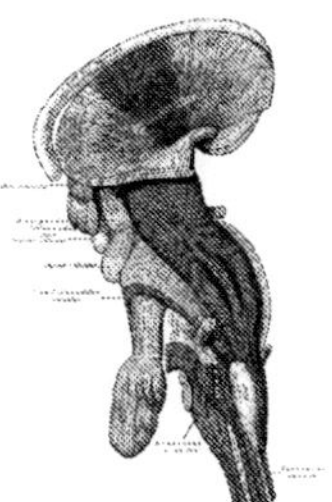
Deep dissection of brain-stem. Lateral view.

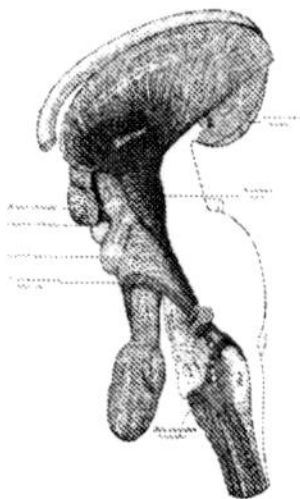
Deep dissection of brain-stem. Lateral view.

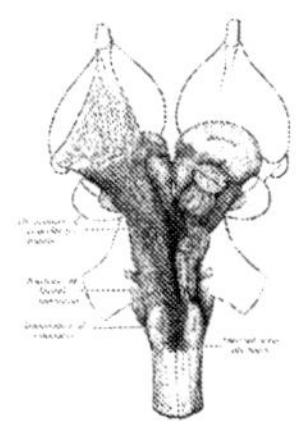
Deep dissection of brain-stem. Ventral view.

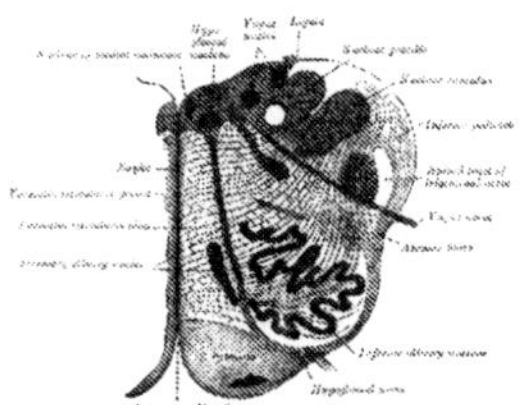
Section of the medulla oblongata at about the middle of the olive.

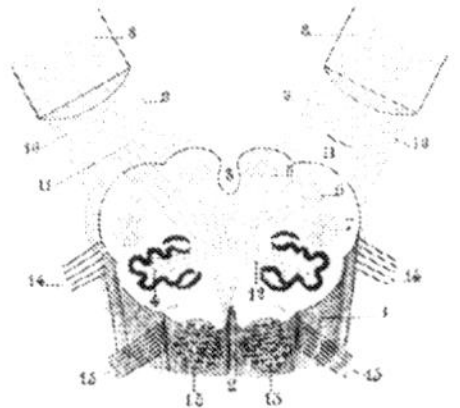
Diagram showing the course of the arcuate fibers.

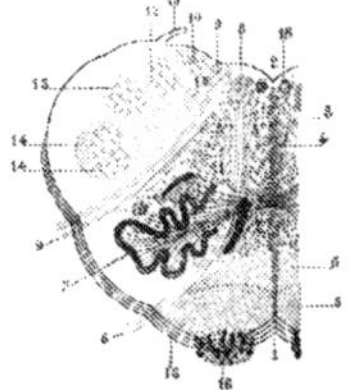
The formatio reticularis of the medulla oblongata, shown by a transverse section passing through the middle of the olive.

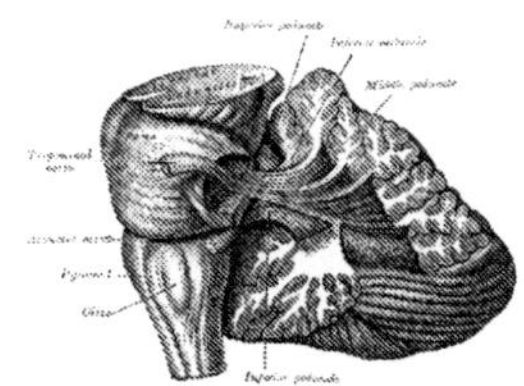
Dissection showing the projection fibers of the cerebellum.

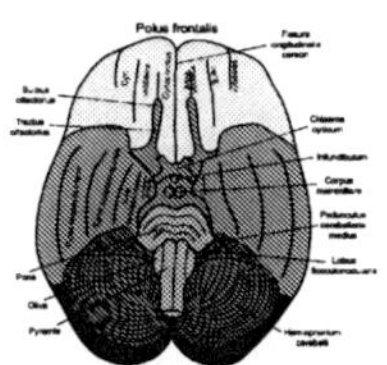
Basal view of a human brain

External links

- Gray's *s187* [3] (primary source for article)
- BrainMaps at UCDavis *Olivary%20nucleus* [4]

This article was originally based on an entry from a public domain edition of Gray's Anatomy. *As such, some of the information contained within it may be outdated.*

Thalamic reticular nucleus

Thalamic reticular nucleus

Brain: Thalamic reticular nucleus	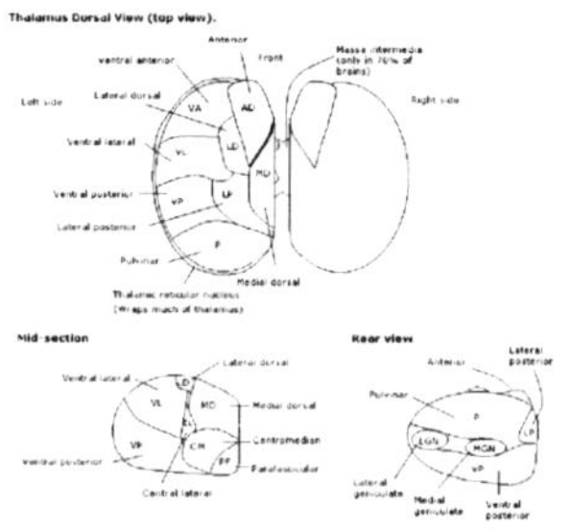
Thalamus	
Latin	*nucleus reticularis thalami*
Part of	Thalamus
NeuroNames	*hier-348* [1]
NeuroLex ID	*birnlex_1721* [2]

The **thalamic reticular nucleus** is part of the ventral thalamus that forms a capsule around the thalamus laterally. However, recent evidence from mice and fish question this statement and define it as dorsal thalamic structure. It is separated from the thalamus by the external medullary lamina. Reticular cells are GABAergic, and have discoid dendritic arbors in the plane of the nucleus.

Thalamic Reticular Nucleus is variously abbreviated TRN, RTN, NRT, and RT.

Input and output

The thalamic reticular nucleus receives input from the cerebral cortex and dorsal thalamic nuclei. Most input comes from collaterals of fibers passing through the thalamic reticular nucleus. Primary thalamic reticular nucleus efferent fibers project to dorsal thalamic nuclei, but never to the cerebral cortex. This is the only thalamic nucleus that does not project to the cerebral cortex, instead it modulates the information from other nuclei in the thalamus. It's function is modulatory on signals going through thalamus (and the reticular nucleus).

It has been suggested that the reticular nucleus receives afferent input from the reticular formation and in turn projects to the other thalamic nuclei , regulating the flow of information through these to the cortex. There is debate over the presence of distinct sectors within the nucleus that each correspond to a different sensory or cognitive modality.

For original connectivity anatomy see Jones 1975.

For discussion of mapping and cross modality pathways see Crabtree 2002.

External links

- BrainMaps at UCDavis *reticular+nucleus+of+thalamus* [3]

Abducens nucleus

Abducens nucleus

Brain: Abducens nucleus	
The cranial nerve nuclei schematically represented; dorsal view. Motor nuclei in red; sensory in blue. The olfactory and optic centers are not represented. (Abducens nucleus is VI)	
Latin	*nucleus nervi abducentis*
Gray's	*subject #187 787* [1]
Part of	Pons
Artery	Pontine branches of the Basilar artery
NeuroNames	*hier-580* [2]
NeuroLex ID	*birnlex_1366* [3]

The **abducens nucleus** is the originating nucleus from which the abducens nerve (VI) emerges - a cranial nerve nucleus. This nucleus is located beneath the fourth ventricle in the caudal portion of the pons, medial to the sulcus limitans.

The abducens nucleus along with the internal genu of the facial nerve make up the facial colliculus, a hump at the caudal end of the medial eminence on the dorsal aspect of the pons.

Clinical significance

Damage to the abducens nucleus causes monocular medial ophthalmoparesis: specifically, loss of the ability to move the ipsilateral eye outward (abduction). This is also seen in damage of the abducens nerve.

In contrast, damage to the area of the **nucleus** can also result in lateral gaze paralysis: loss of the ability to move either eye in the direction of the side with the lesion. This is due to damage to both the motoneurons and interneurons projecting through the medial longitudinal fasciculus to the contralateral medial rectus neurons.

Additional images

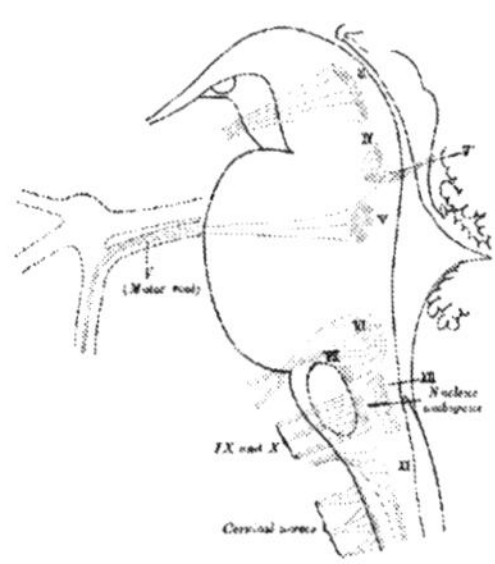
Nuclei of origin of cranial motor nerves schematically represented; lateral view.

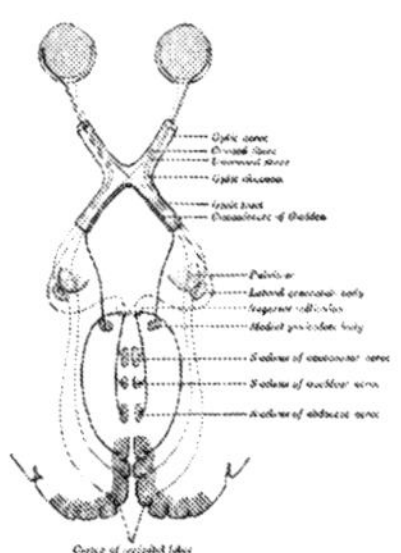
Scheme showing central connections of the optic nerves and optic tracts.

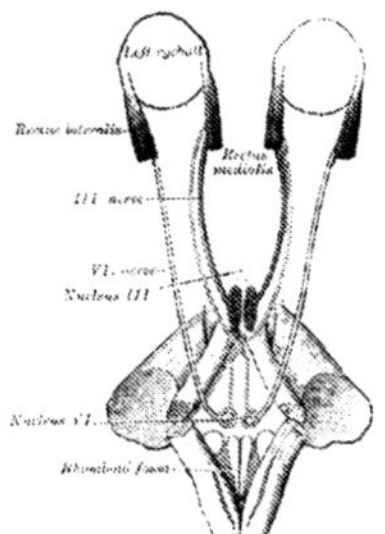
Figure showing the mode of innervation of the Recti medialis and lateralis of the eye.

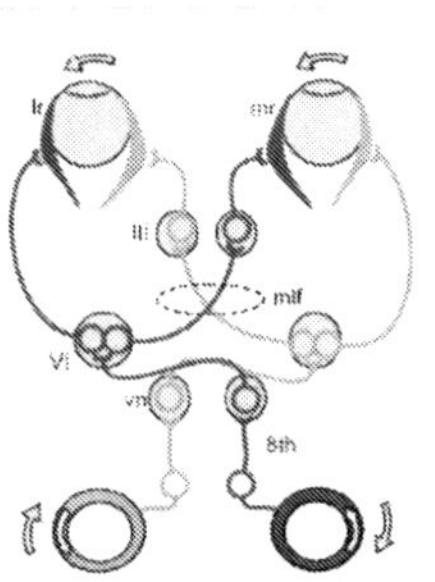

Vestibulo-ocular reflex

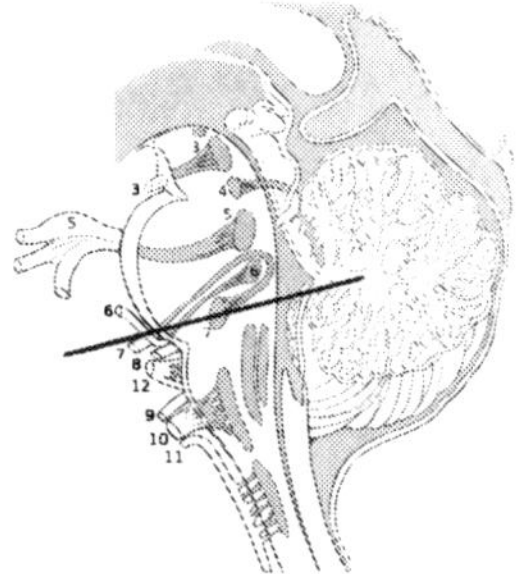
Brain stem sagittal section

External links

- Brainstem at UWisc *13VNAN* [4]
- MedEd at Loyola *Neuro/frames/nlBSs/nl27fr.htm* [5]
- Template (look for "GSE") [6]
- BrainMaps at UCDavis *Abducens nucleus* [7]
- NIF Search - Abducens Nucleus [8] via the Neuroscience Information Framework

Pontine nuclei

Pontine nuclei

Brain: Pontine nuclei	
Latin	*nuclei pontis*
Gray's	*subject #187 786* [1]
NeuroNames	*hier-613* [2]

The **pontine nuclei** are a part of the pons which store the memory of intention during motor activity. Corticopontine fibres carry information from the primary motor cortex to the ipsilateral pontine nucleus in the ventral pons, and the pontocerebellar projection then carries that information to the contralateral cerebellum via the middle cerebellar peduncle.

They therefore allow modification of actions in the light of their outcome, or error correction, and are hence important in learning motor skills.

External links

- Neuroanatomy at UW *Bs97/TEXT/P16/intro.htm* [3]
- Diagram at mindsci-clinic.com [4]

Rhombencephalon

Rhombencephalon

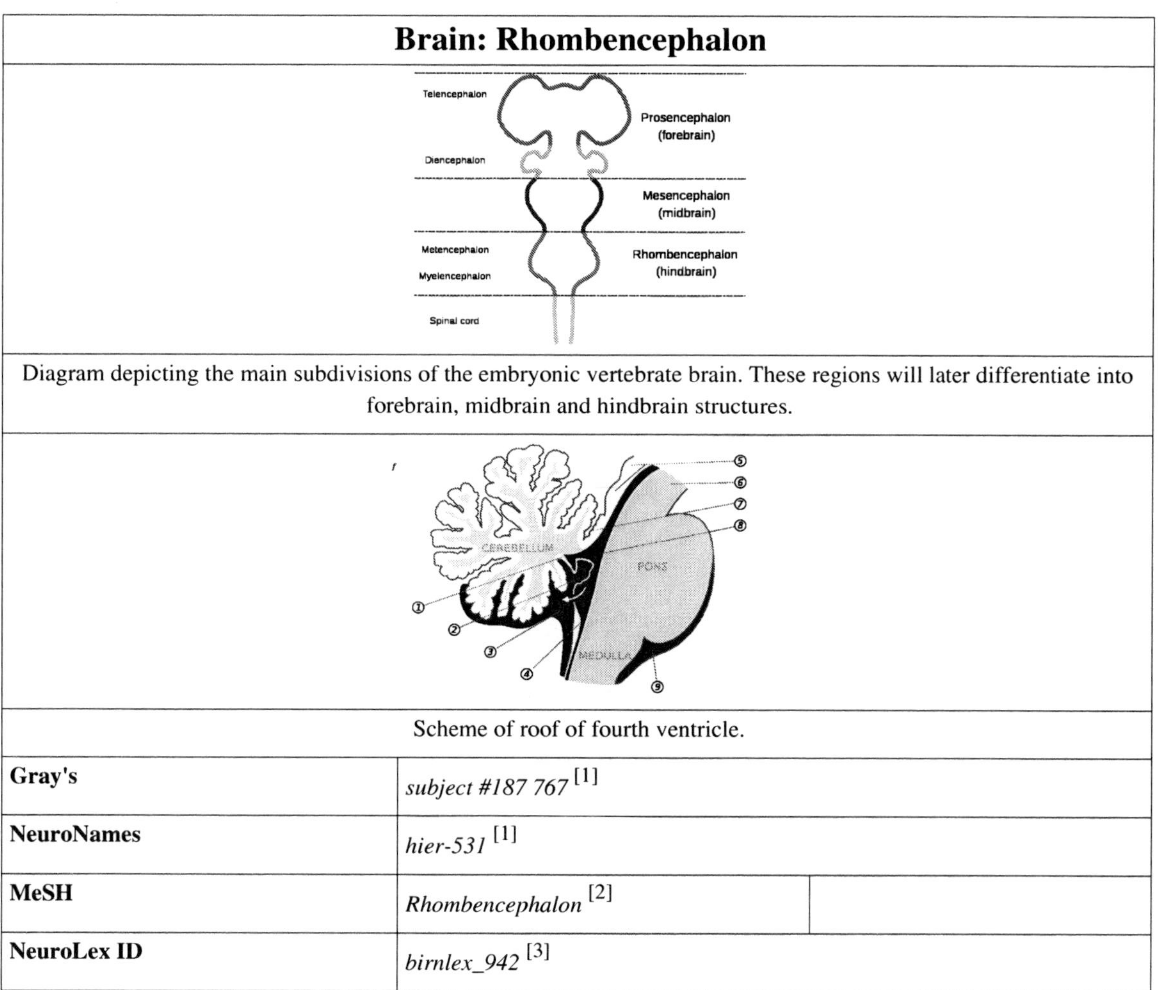

Brain: Rhombencephalon	
Diagram depicting the main subdivisions of the embryonic vertebrate brain. These regions will later differentiate into forebrain, midbrain and hindbrain structures.	
Scheme of roof of fourth ventricle.	
Gray's	*subject #187 767* [1]
NeuroNames	*hier-531* [1]
MeSH	*Rhombencephalon* [2]
NeuroLex ID	*birnlex_942* [3]

The **rhombencephalon** (or **hindbrain**) is a developmental categorization of portions of the central nervous system in vertebrates.

The rhombencephalon can be subdivided in a variable number of transversal swellings called rhombomeres. In the human embryo eight rhombomeres can be distinguished, from caudal to rostral: Rh7-Rh1 and the isthmus (the most rostral rhombomere).

A rare disease of the rhombencephalon, "rhombencephalosynapsis" is characterized by a missing vermis resulting in a fused cerebellum. Patients generally present with cerebellar ataxia.

The caudal rhombencephalon has been generally considered as the initiation site for neural tube closure.

Myelencephalon

Rhombomeres Rh7-Rh4 form the myelencephalon.

The myelencephalon forms the medulla oblongata in the adult brain; it contains:

- a portion of the fourth ventricle,
- the glossopharyngeal nerve (CN IX),
- vagus nerve (CN X),
- accessory nerve (CN XI),
- hypoglossal nerve (CN XII),
- and a portion of the vestibulocochlear nerve (CN VIII).

Metencephalon

Rhombomeres Rh3-Rh1 form the metencephalon.

The metencephalon is composed of the pons and the cerebellum; it contains:

- a portion of the fourth ventricle,
- the trigeminal nerve (CN V),
- abducens nerve (CN VI),
- facial nerve (CN VII),
- and a portion of the vestibulocochlear nerve (CN VIII).

Additional images

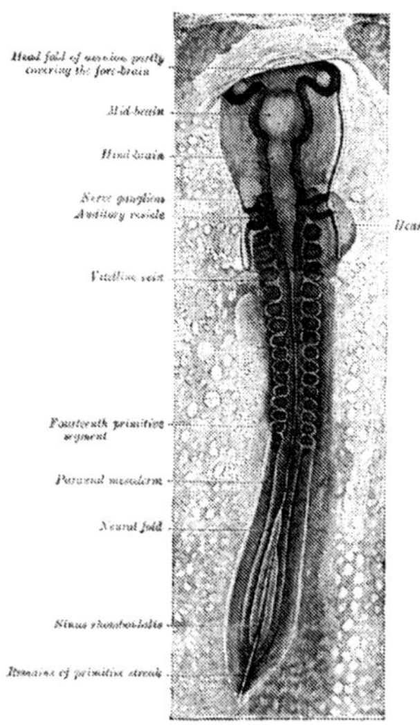

Chick embryo of thirty-three hours' incubation, viewed from the dorsal aspect. X 30.

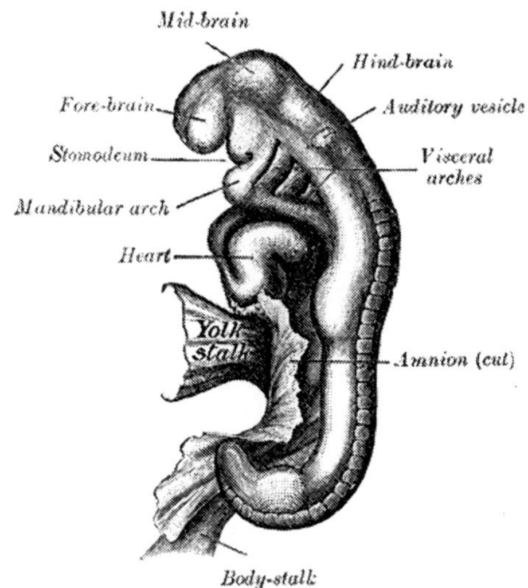

Embryo between eighteen and twenty-one days.

External links

- NIF Search - Rhombencephalon [4] via the Neuroscience Information Framework

Metencephalon

Metencephalon

Brain: Metencephalon

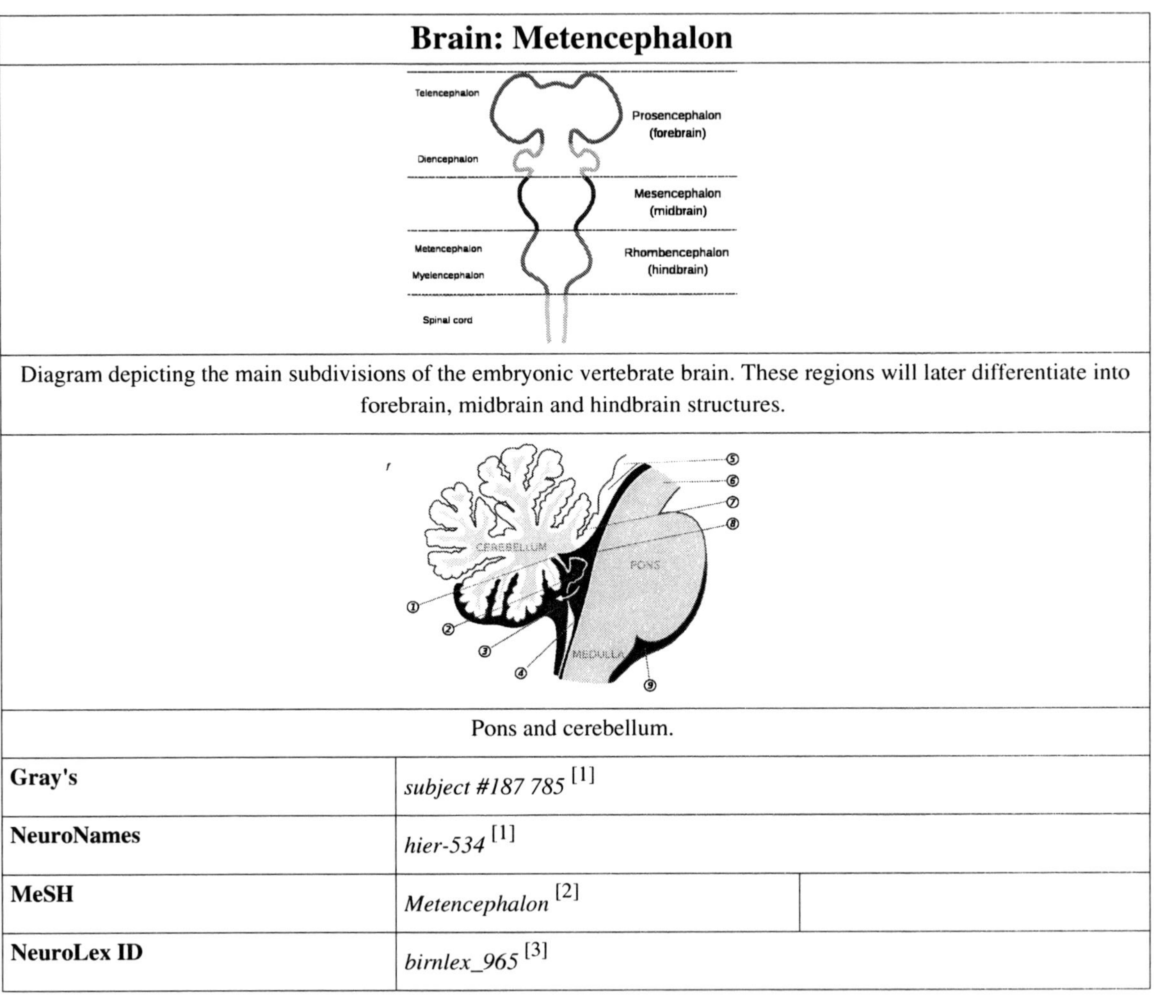

Diagram depicting the main subdivisions of the embryonic vertebrate brain. These regions will later differentiate into forebrain, midbrain and hindbrain structures.

Pons and cerebellum.

Gray's	*subject #187 785* [1]	
NeuroNames	*hier-534* [1]	
MeSH	*Metencephalon* [2]	
NeuroLex ID	*birnlex_965* [3]	

The **metencephalon** is a developmental categorization of portions of the central nervous system. The metencephalon is composed of the pons and the cerebellum; contains a portion of the fourth ventricle; and the trigeminal nerve (CN V), abducens nerve (CN VI), facial nerve (CN VII), and a portion of the vestibulocochlear nerve (CN VIII).

The metencephalon develops from the hindbrain, and is differentiated from the myelencephalon in the embryo by approximately 5 weeks of age. By the third month, the metencephalon differentiates into its two main structures, the pons and the cerebellum.

The pons regulates breathing through particular nuclei that regulate the breathing center of the medulla oblongata. The cerebellum works to coordinate muscle movements, maintain posture, and integrate sensory information from the inner ear and proprioceptors in the muscles and joints.

See also

List of regions in the human brain

Climbing fiber

Climbing fiber

Neuron: Climbing fiber

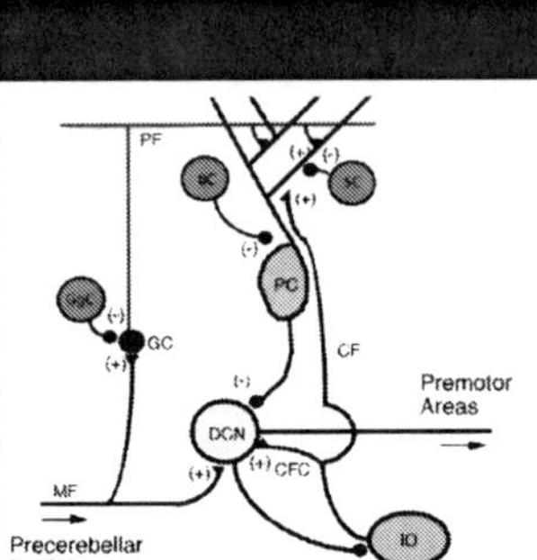

Microcircuitry of the cerebellum. Excitatory synapses are denoted by (+) and inhibitory synapses by (-). Climbing fiber is shown originating from the inferior olive (green).

Location	Inferior Olive and Cerebellum
Function	Unique excitatory function (see text)
Morphology	Unique projection neuron (see text)
Presynaptic connections	Inferior olive
Postsynaptic connections	Purkinje cells
Gray's	*subject #187 796* [1]

Climbing fibers are the name given to a series of neuronal projections from the inferior olivary nucleus located in the medulla oblongata.

These axons pass through the pons and enter the cerebellum via the inferior cerebellar peduncle where they form synapses with the deep cerebellar nuclei and Purkinje cells. Each climbing fiber will form synapses with 1-10 Purkinje cells.

Early in development, Purkinje cells are innervated by multiple climbing fibers, but as the cerebellum matures, these inputs gradually become eliminated resulting in a single climbing fiber input per Purkinje cell.

These fibers provide very powerful, excitatory input to the cerebellum which results in the generation of complex spike excitatory postsynaptic potential (EPSP) in Purkinje cells. In this way climbing fibers (CFs) perform a central role in motor behaviors.

Climbing fiber activation is thought to serve as a motor error signal sent to the cerebellum, and is an important signal for motor timing.

These climbing fibers carry information from various sources such as the spinal cord, vestibular system, red nucleus, superior colliculus, reticular formation and sensory and motor cortices.

See also

- Axon terminals
- Parallel fiber

External links

- Climbing Fiber Discharge Regulates Cerebellar Functions by Controlling the intrinsic Characteristics of Purkinje Cell Output [2]
- Spatiotemporal Tuning of Optic Flow Inputs to the Vestibulocerebellum in Pigeons: Differences Between Mossy and Climbing Fiber Pathways [3]

Apneustic respirations

Apneustic respirations

Apneustic respiration (a.k.a. **apneusis**) is an abnormal pattern of breathing characterized by deep, gasping inspiration with a pause at full inspiration followed by a brief, insufficient release.

Accompanying signs and symptoms may include decerebrate posturing; fixed, dilated pupils; coma or profound stupor; quadriparesis; absent corneal reflex; absent doll's eye sign; negative oculocephalic reflex; and obliteration of the gag reflex.

Causes

It is caused by damage to the pons or upper medulla caused by strokes or trauma. Specifically, concurrent removal of input from the vagus nerve and the pneumotaxic center causes this pattern of breathing. It is an ominous sign, with a generally poor prognosis.

It can also be temporarily caused by some drugs, such as ketamine.

See also

- Apneustic center

External links

- About brain injury and functions [1]
- http://jap.physiology.org/cgi/reprint/55/3/851.pdf
- *912982089* [2] at GPnotebook

Corpora quadrigemina

Corpora quadrigemina

Brain: Corpora quadrigemina		
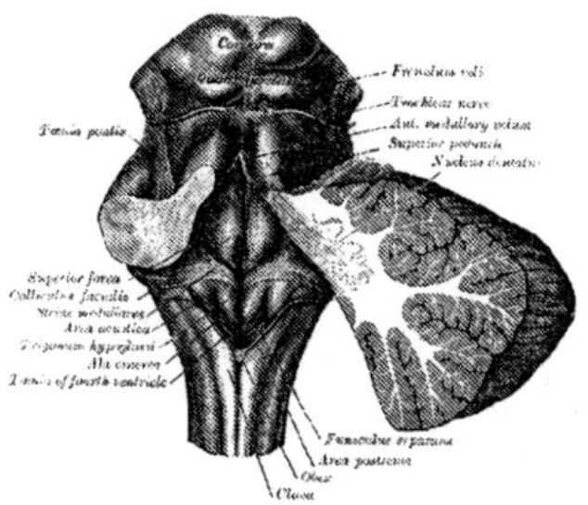		
Rhomboid fossa. ("Corpora quadrigemina" visible at top).		
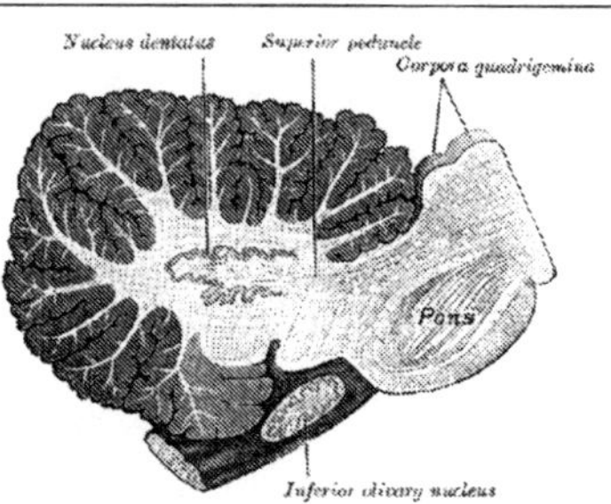		
Sagittal section through right cerebellar hemisphere. The right olive has also been cut sagittally. ("Corpora quadrigemina" visible at upper right).		
Gray's	*subject #188 805* [1]	
NeuroNames	*ancil-324* [1]	
MeSH	*Corpora+Quadrigemina* [2]	

In the brain, the **corpora quadrigemina** (Latin for "quadruplet bodies") are the four colliculi—two inferior, two superior—located on the tectum the dorsal aspect of the midbrain.

The corpora quadrigemina are reflex centers involving vision and hearing.

Additional images

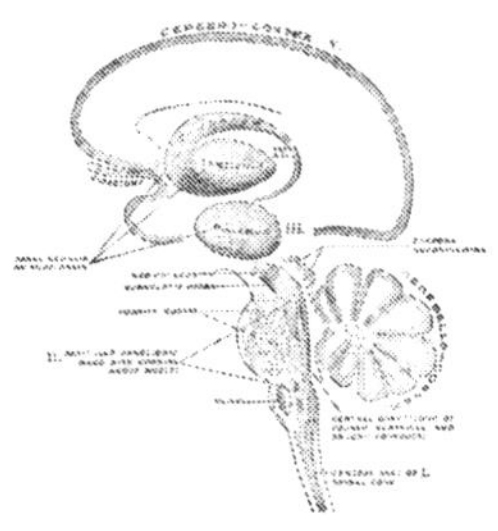
Schematic representation of the chief ganglionic categories (I to V).

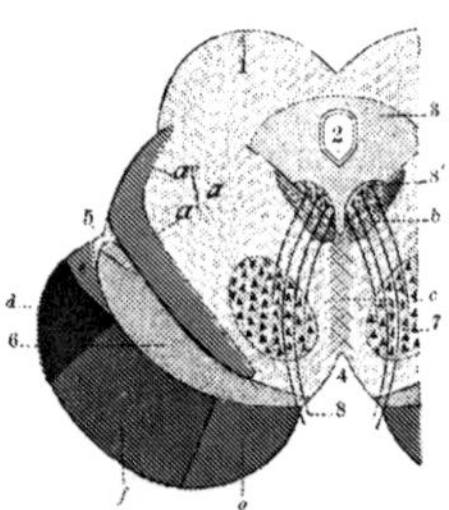
Coronal section through mid-brain.

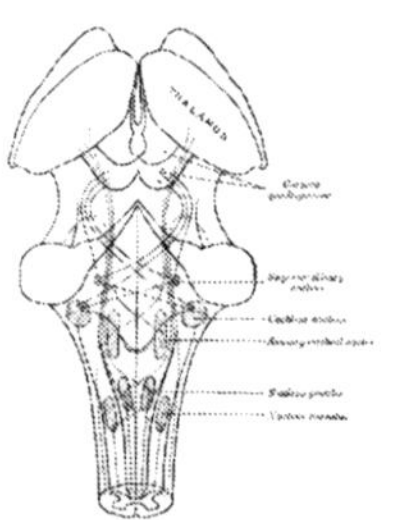
Scheme showing the course of the fibers of the lemniscus; medial lemniscus in blue, lateral in red.

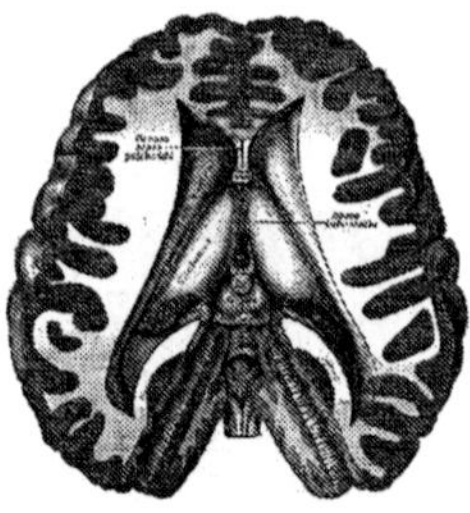
Dissection showing the ventricles of the brain.

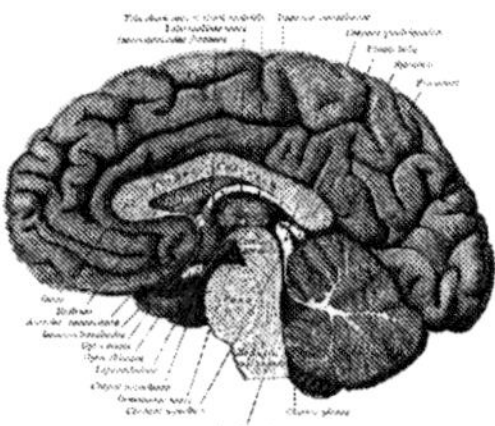
Median sagittal section of brain.

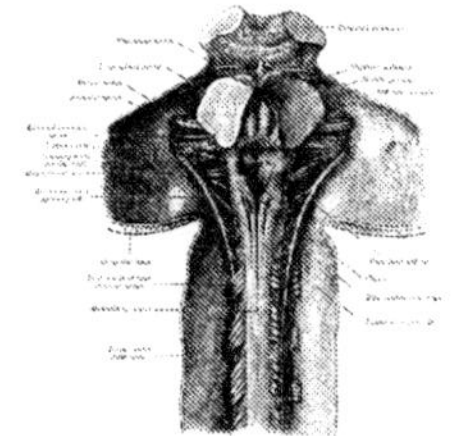
Upper part of medulla spinalis and hind- and mid-brains; posterior aspect, exposed in situ.

External links

- SUNY Niagara [3]
- Diagram [4]

Accessory cuneate nucleus

Accessory cuneate nucleus

<table>
<tr><th colspan="2">Brain: Accessory cuneate nucleus</th></tr>
<tr><td colspan="2">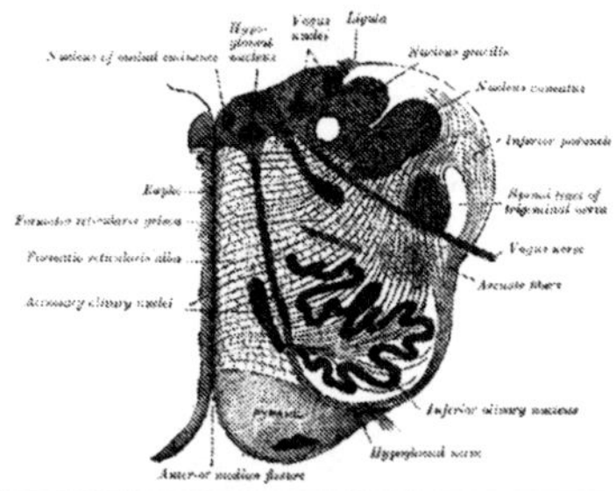</td></tr>
<tr><td colspan="2">Section of the medulla oblongata at about the middle of the olive. (Accessory cuneate nucleus is not labeled, but cuneate nucleus is labeled at upper right, and the accessory cuneate nucleus would be found lateral to it.)</td></tr>
<tr><td>Latin</td><td>nucleus cuneatus accessorius</td></tr>
<tr><td>Part of</td><td>Medulla oblongata</td></tr>
<tr><td>NeuroNames</td><td>hier-765 [1]</td></tr>
<tr><td>NeuroLex ID</td><td>birnlex_2634 [2]</td></tr>
</table>

The **accessory cuneate nucleus** is located lateral to the cuneate nucleus in the medulla oblongata at the level of the sensory decussation (the crossing fibers of the posterior column/medial lemniscus tract).

It receives input from cervical spinal nerves and transmits that information to the cerebellum.

These fibers are called cuneocerebellar (cuneate nucleus > cerebellum) fibers.

In this function, the accessory cuneate nucleus is comparable to the upper extremity portion of the posterior spinocerebellar tract.

External links

- NIF Search - Accessory Cuneate Nucleus [3] via the Neuroscience Information Framework

Zona incerta

Zona incerta

Brain: Zona incerta	
Gray's	*subject #189 812* [1]
NeuroNames	*hier-421* [2]

The **zona incerta** is a horizontally elongated region of gray matter cells in the subthalamus below the thalamus. Its connections project extensively over the brain from the cerebral cortex down into the spinal cord.

Its function is unknown though several have been proposed related to "limbic–motor integration" such as controlling visceral activity and pain; gating sensory input and synchronizing cortical and subcortical brain rhythms. Its dysfunction may play a role in central pain syndrome. It is also been identified as a promising deep brain stimulation therapy target for treating Parkinsons Disease.

Its existence was first described by Auguste Forel in 1877 as a "region of which nothing certain can be said". A hundred and thirty years later in 2007, Nadia Urbain and Martin Deschênes of Université Laval noted that the "zona incerta is among the least studied regions of the brain; its name does not even appear in the index of many textbooks."

Anatomy

This nucleus is located medially to the internal capsule, ventral to the thalamus, and is contiguous with the thalamic reticular nucleus. The nucleus separates the lenticular fasciculus from the thalamic fasciculus (also known as the "field H1 of Forel") . Its cells are very heterogeneous differing widely in their shape and size. Its chemoarchitecture is also diverse containing up to 20 different types of neurochemically defined cells. It has been noted that "There are few diencephalic regions that have as much cellular and neurochemical diversity".

In rats four areas are usually identified.

- a rostral sector that has densely packed spindle-shaped cells and scattered larger oval shaped cells.
- a dorsal sector that has medium-sized oval-shaped cells.

- a ventral sector made up of medium-sized multipolar or fusiform shaped cells that are more densely packed than the cells in the dorsal sector
- a caudal sector made up of small and medium-sized somata that are either multipolar, fusiform or rounded in shape, together with a group of very large multipolar-shaped cells located medially. This is sometimes called the motor part of the zona incerta nucleus. This is the area targeted by deep brain stimulation area when the zona incerta is targeted in the treatment of Parkinson Disease.

These areas lack clear cell-free borders and merge into each other.

Zona incerta neurons have dendrites with a wide span 0.8 mm and their axons give off collaterals that arborized locally within the zona incerta providing a means for lateral inhibition. The ventral area of the zona incerta has been described as having "a network of GABAergic cells with widespread interconnections, so that cells in one subsector may influence the activity of cells in a different subsector".

The zona incerta together with the hypothalamus is one of the two areas of the brain that produces the neuropeptide melanin concentrating hormone. Dopaminergic ones are also more prevalent. There are in addition populations of cells producing somatostatin, angiotensin II and melanocyte stimulating hormone.

Connections

The zona incerta has connections to the cerebral cortex, diencephalon, basal ganglia, brainstem and spinal cord.

Cerebral cortex

Projections to the zona incerta arise across the cortical mantel from the frontal to the occipital lobes. The heaviest projections are from cingulate cortex, frontal and parietal areas. The head area of the body seems from these areas to have the largest representation in the zona incerta. These projections preferentially go to cortical layer I neurons. There are projections from the zona incerta back to the cerebral cortex.

Diencephalon

Projections with the diencephalon are reciprocal and mainly to the thalamus such as the intralaminar nucleus (parafascicular nucleus and central lateral nucleus) and higher-order nuclei such as the lateral posterior nucleus. The zona incerta avoids the thalamus nuclei of the primary sensory areas such as the ventral posterior nucleus of the somatosensory system and the lateral geniculate of the visual system.

Hypothalamus

Projections to the hypothalamus go mainly to the paraventricular nucleus areas in the anterior hypothalamus, lateral hypothalamus, lateral preoptic area, horizontal diagonal band of Broca, and the parvocellular region of the paraventricular nucleus.

Basal ganglia

Zona incerta is connected in the basal ganglia to the substantia nigra (both pars compacta and pars reticulata) and pedunculopontine tegmental nucleus (but only its pars dissipata area). It also has less important connections to the entopeduncular nucleus and globus pallidus. These projections are glutamatergic and excitatory rather than GABAergic and inhibitory. The zona incerta also receives input from these areas.

Brainstem

Zona incerta receives input from many parts of the brainstem nuclei including the periaqueductal gray, raphe nuclei, thalamic reticular nucleus, and the deep layers of the superior colliculus. It is regulated by inputs from brainstem cholinergic nuclei such as the Laterodorsal tegmental nucleus and pedunculopontine nucleus upon its neuron's muscarinic receptors.

Spinal cord

Zona incerta afferents terminate within the spinal cord gray matter, particularly the anterior horn, while spinal projections back to the zona incerta arise from cells located across the posterior horn and intermediate gray.

Other

Zona incerta also has connections to the amygdala, basal forebrain, the osmoreceptors in the subfornical organ, olfactory bulb, posterior pituitary and habenula.

Some of these projections appear in register; the representation of the same body part in cortex and spinal cord connect to the same areas in the zona incerta. This is possibly so with the superior colliculus.

Functions

The function of the Zona incerta is unknown, "To this day, we are still not certain of the precise function of this 'zone of uncertainty'" However it is suggested to have possible roles in "limbic–motor integration".

Visceral survival activities.

Zona incerta controls such activities as water and food intake, sexuality and cardiovascular activity. This control is related to its effects upon the nearby posterior hypothalamus with which it shares similar connections and neurochemically defined cell types.

The zona incerta receives pain input through the spinothalamic tract and this has been shown to control the activity of the pain transmission pathway in the posterior thalamus.

Electrical or chemical stimulation of the zona incerta creates limbic-related movements, such as those associated with defense orientation and copulation.

Sensory-motor activities.

At rest sensory input to the higher sensory areas of the cerebral cortex is gated through the thalamus. It has moreover been proposed that the zona incerta provides a top-down disinhibitory mechanism of this gating when there is sensory-motor activity such as the tactile use of whiskers.

This has also been linked to sensory gating changes between sleep and waking. In this occurs a zona incerta mediated inhibition of thalamic nuclei such the somatosensory posterior medial thalamus. This is most strong when cholinergic input to the zona incerta is reduced as during slow-wave sleep and during anesthesia. The consequence of this has been explained upon information processing:

> As a result, posterior medial thalamus neurons fail to respond to ascending sensory inputs, and function primarily in "higher-order" mode, concerned with relaying trans-cortical information. By contrast, increased cholinergic activity during wakefulness and enhanced vigilance suppresses zona incerta -mediated inhibition, thereby ungating posterior thalamus responses to ascending inputs.

The zona incerta projects to the superior colliculus and these link to the initiation of orientating eye and head movements. In monkeys for example neuronal activity in the zona incerta "pauses" before the start of a saccade and resumes at the end of a saccade.

Synchronizing cortical and subcortical brain rhythms and integration.

The GABAergic input received from the cerebral cortex has been suggested to synchronize thalamocortical and brainstem rhythms by providing a link between basal ganglia output and the cerebello-thalamo cortical loop. This allows it to synchronize oscillations generate by the basal ganglia during the preparation and execution of intended movements. One function of the loop is to carry movement instructions to the motor cortex through zona incerta output to the ventral lateral nucleus neurons in the cerebello-thalamocortical loop and to brainstem motor neurons in the medial reticular formation and midbrain extrapyramidal area. This acts to synchronize the basal ganglia areas involved in planning and execution of the movement with those in the brainstem controlling axial and proximal limb muscles with those areas in the motor cortex that control distal limb movements.

Synthesis

John Mitrofanis at the University of Sydney has proposed a general theory that might underlie some of the above.

> The zona incerta is in a position to form a primal synaptic interface of the diencephalon, linking diverse sensory channels to appropriate visceral, arousal, attention and posture-locomotion responses. The different sensory inputs, whether exteroreceptive (somatic) or interoreceptive (visceral), influence these activities by driving zona incerta cells with different projection patterns and functions; each of these cells may be located in different sectors of the zone... In essence, it is suggested that the zona incerta has the pathways to integrate both exteroreceptive (e.g. somatosensory) and interoreceptive (e.g. thirst) sensory challenges, so that visceral activity, arousal, attention and/or posture

locomotion are altered and/or generated. The zona incerta could form a neural niche in the thalamus from where these responses are "recruited" immediately, as to give an instant response.

Parkinsons Disease

Parkinsons Disease might disrupt the zona incerta as it is hyperactive in parkinsonian experimental animals. In humans with Parkinsons Disease, surgical lesion of the zona incerta alleviates their parkinsonian motor symptoms.

Deep brain stimulation of the subthalamic nucleus in those with Parkinson Disease has identified the zona incerta as a promising target area for effective therapy. Unlike deep bilateral stimulation of the ventral lateral nucleus such stimulation of the zona incerta improves all aspects of tremor including both the distal and proximal parts of limbs and the body more generally. This also occurs without dysarthria and disequilibrium as this stimulation does not interrupt proprioceptive sensation and the processing of the fine motor skill movements of vocal cords.

Researchers observed that "The ventral lateral nucleus has long been established as an effective surgical target for controlling distal limb tremor, including Parkinson Disease tremor. However, because it receives predominantly cerebellar afferents and no direct basal ganglia afferents, the reason why it is effective in controlling Parkinson Disease tremor has remained a paradox. The conduction of abnormal oscillations generated in the basal ganglia in Parkinson Disease to the ventral lateral nucleus via zona incerta would therefore explain this paradox and also explain why we observed such a potent anti-tremor effect from stimulating zona incerta in our patients with Parkinson Disease"

The study further noted that deep brain stimulation upon the zona incerta "is effective in suppressing all components of tremor affecting both the distal and proximal part of the body. These results, if replicated in larger randomised controlled studies, have important implications for our current surgical management of patients with tremor and point to a more promising target area than the ventral lateral nucleus of the thalamus."

Central pain syndrome

Central pain syndrome is pain initiated or caused by injury or dysfunction in the central nervous system. Recent research suggests that the development and maintenance of such pain could link to abnormal inhibitory regulation by the zona incerta of the posterior thalamus. It has been suggested that there exists

> a significant suppression of both spontaneous and evoked activity in inhibitory neurons in zona incerta and abnormally high spontaneous and evoked activity of neurons in posterior thalamus in animals with central pain syndrome. The positive association between behavioral and neurophysiological thresholds in rats with central pain syndrome is

consistent with a causal role for suppressed incerto-thalamic inputs in central pain syndrome.

External links

- BrainMaps at UCDavis *zona+incerta* [3]
- http://isc.temple.edu/neuroanatomy/lab/atlas/pdhn/

Obex

Obex

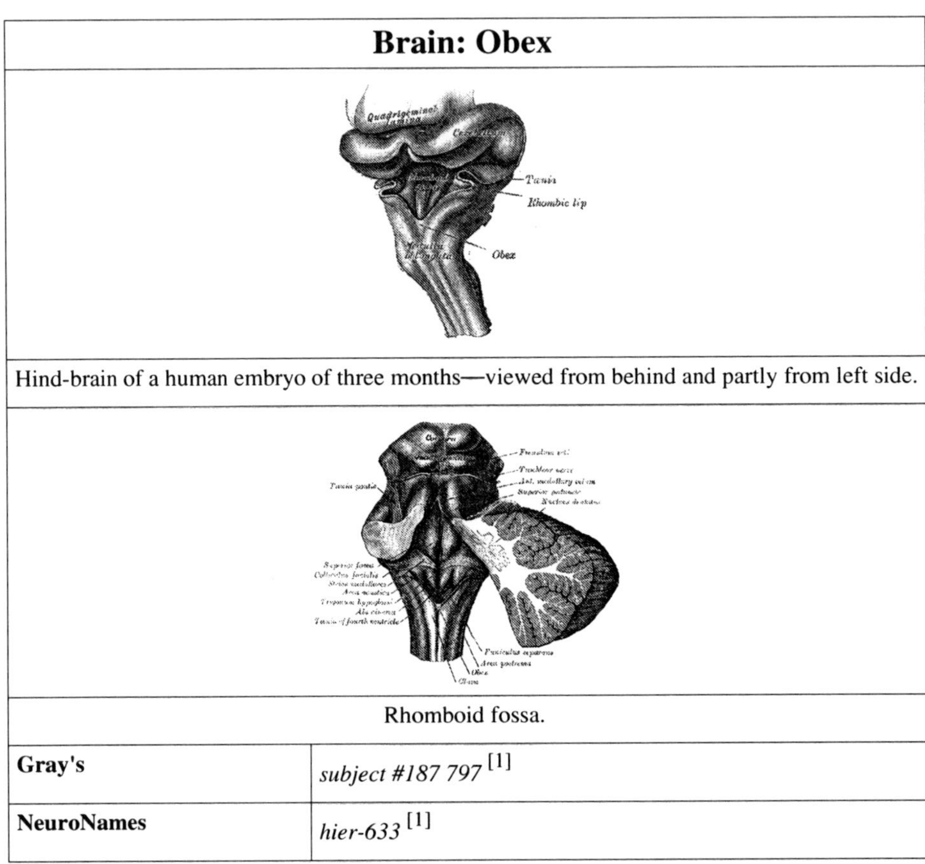

Brain: Obex	
Hind-brain of a human embryo of three months—viewed from behind and partly from left side.	
Rhomboid fossa.	
Gray's	*subject #187 797* [1]
NeuroNames	*hier-633* [1]

The **obex** (from the Latin for *barrier*) is the point in the human brain at which the fourth ventricle narrows to become the central canal of the spinal cord.

The obex occurs in the caudal medulla.

The decussating of sensory fibers happens at this point.

Clinical significance

Hemangioblastoma has been observed in this location.

External links

- Photo at aphis.usda.gov [2] (file not found as of 2008-08-16)

Paramedian pontine reticular formation

Paramedian pontine reticular formation

Brain: Paramedian pontine reticular formation	
Axial section of the pons at the level of the facial colliculus (PPRF not labeled, but region is visible, near abducens nucleus)	
NeuroNames	*ancil-479* [1]

The **paramedian pontine reticular formation**, or **PPRF**, is part of the pontine reticular formation, a brain region without clearly defined borders in the center of the pons. It is involved in the coordination of eye movements, particularly horizontal gaze and saccades.

Inputs, outputs, functions

The PPRF is located anterior and lateral to the medial longitudinal fasciculus (MLF). It receives input from the superior colliculus via the predorsal bundle and from the frontal eye fields via frontopontine fibers. The rostral PPRF probably coordinates vertical saccades; the caudal PPRF may be the generator of horizontal saccades. In particular, activity of the excitatory burst neurons (EBNs) in the PPRF generates the "pulse" movement that initiates a saccade. In the case of horizontal saccades the "pulse" information is conveyed via axonal fibers to the abducens nucleus, initiating lateral eye movements. The angular velocity of the eye during horizontal saccade ranges from 100 to 700 degrees per second. Larger saccades have faster pulses; the PPRF is involved in this determination.[Brazis]

Lesions

Unilateral lesions of the PPRF produce characteristic findings:[Zee]

- Loss of horizontal saccades directed towards the side of the lesion, no matter the current position of gaze
- Contralateral gaze deviation (acute lesions, such as early stroke, only)
- Gaze-evoked lateral nystagmus on looking away from the side of the lesion
- Bilateral lesions produce horizontal gaze palsy and slowing of vertical saccades

See also

- Internuclear ophthalmoplegia
- Multiple sclerosis
- One and a half syndrome
- Ophthalmoparesis
- Reticular formation
- Stroke
- Paramedian reticular nucleus
- Opsoclonus
- Saccade

References

1. Brazis, P.W., Masdeu, J.C., and Biller, J. *Localization in Clinical Neurology*, 4th edition. Lippincott, Williams, and Wilkins, Philadelphia, 2001; pp. 213-216. ISBN 0-7817-2843-6
2. Adapted from Leigh, R.J., and Zee, D.S. *The Neurology of Eye Movements*, 3rd edition. Oxford University Press, Oxford, England, 1999; p. 499. ISBN 0-19-512972-5

Facial motor nucleus

Facial motor nucleus

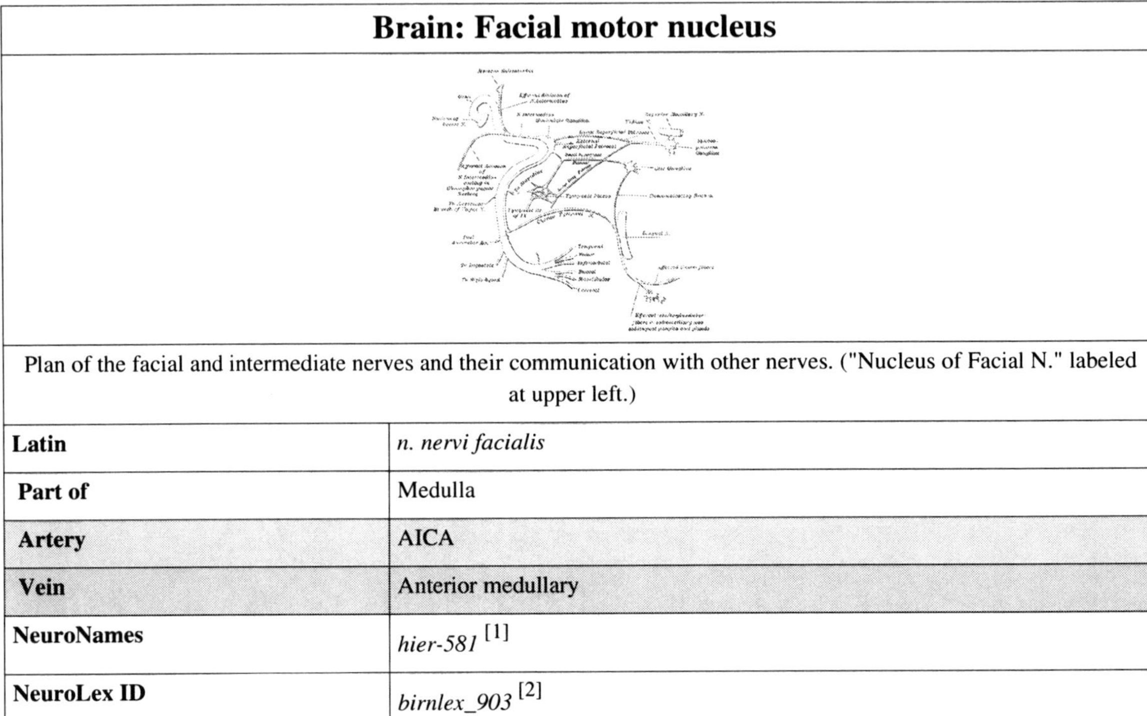

Brain: Facial motor nucleus	
Plan of the facial and intermediate nerves and their communication with other nerves. ("Nucleus of Facial N." labeled at upper left.)	
Latin	*n. nervi facialis*
Part of	Medulla
Artery	AICA
Vein	Anterior medullary
NeuroNames	*hier-581* [1]
NeuroLex ID	*birnlex_903* [2]

The **facial motor nucleus** is a collection of neurons in the brainstem that belong to the facial nerve (cranial nerve VII). These lower motor neurons innervate the muscles of facial expression and the stapedius.

Anatomy

The nucleus is situated in the caudal portion of the ventrolateral pontine tegmentum. Its axons take an unusual course, traveling dorsally and looping around the abducens nucleus, then traveling ventrally to exit the ventral pons medial to the spinal trigeminal nucleus. These axons form the motor component of the facial nerve, with parasympathetic and sensory components forming the nervus intermedius.

The nucleus has a dorsal and ventral region, with neurons in the dorsal region innervating muscles of the upper face and neurons in the ventral region innervating muscles of the lower face.

Classification

Because it innervates muscles derived from pharyngeal arches, the facial motor nucleus is considered part of the special visceral efferent (SVE) cell column, which also includes the trigeminal motor nucleus, nucleus ambiguus, and (arguably) the spinal accessory nucleus.

Cortical input

Like all lower motor neurons, cells of the facial motor nucleus receive cortical input from the primary motor cortex in the frontal lobe of the brain. Upper motor neurons of the cortex send axons that descend through the internal capsule and synapse on neurons in the facial motor nucleus. This pathway from the cortex to the brainstem is called the corticobulbar tract.

Interestingly, the neurons in the dorsal aspect of the facial motor nucleus receive inputs from both sides of the cortex, while those in the ventral aspect mainly receive contralateral inputs (i.e. from the opposite side of the cortex). The result is that both sides of the brain control the muscles of the upper face, while the right side of the brain controls the lower left side of the face, and the left side of the brain controls the lower right side of the face.

Effects of lesions

As a result of the corticobulbar input to the facial motor nucleus, an upper motor neuron lesion to fibers innervating the facial motor nucleus results in central seven. The syndrome is characterized by spastic paralysis of the contralateral lower face. For example, a left corticobulbar lesion results in paralysis of the muscles that control the lower right quadrant of the face.

By contrast, a lower motor neuron lesion to the facial motor nucleus results in paralysis of facial muscles on the same side of the injury. If a cause, such as trauma or infection, cannot be identified (this situation is called idiopathic palsy) this condition is known as Bell's palsy. Otherwise it is described by its cause.

MECHANISM of Facial Nerve Upper vs Lower Motor Neuron Lesions:

Any lesion occurring within or affecting the corticobulbar tract is known as an upper motor neuron lesion. Any lesion affecting the individual branches (temporal, zygomatic, buccal, mandibular and cervical) is known as a lower motor neuron lesion.

Branches of the facial nerve leaving the facial motor nucleus (FMN) for the muscles do so via both left and right posterior (dorsal) and anterior (ventral) routes. In other words, this means lower motor neurons of the facial nerve can leave either from the left anterior, left posterior, right anterior or right posterior facial motor nucleus. The temporal branch travels out from the left and right posterior components. The inferior four branches do so via the left and right anterior components. The left and right branches supply their respective sides of the face (ipsilateral innervation). Accordingly, the posterior components receive motor input from both hemispheres of the cerebral cortex (bilaterally), whereas the anterior components receive strictly contralateral input. This means that the temporal branch of the facial nerve receives motor input from both hemispheres of the cerebral cortex whereas the zygomatic, buccal, mandibular and cervical branches receive information from only contralateral hemispheres.

Now, because the anterior FMN receives only contralateral cortical input whereas the posterior receives that which is bilateral, a corticobulbar lesion (UMN lesion) occurring in the left hemisphere would eliminate motor input to the right anterior FMN component, thus removing signaling to the inferior four facial nerve branches, thereby paralyzing the right mid- and lower-face. The posterior component, however, although now only receiving input from the right hemisphere, is still able to allow the temporal branch to sufficiently innervate the entire forehead. This means that the forehead will not be paralyzed.

The same mechanism applies for an upper motor neuron lesion in the right hemisphere. The left anterior FMN component no longer receives cortical motor input due to its strict contralateral innervation, whereas the posterior component is still sufficiently supplied by the left hemisphere. The result is paralysis of the left mid- and lower-face with an unaffected forehead.

On the other hand, a lower motor neuron lesion is a bit different.

A lesion on either the left or right side would affect both the anterior and posterior routes on that side because of their close physical proximity to one another. So, a lesion on the left side would inhibit muscle innervation from both the left posterior and anterior routes, thus paralyzing the whole left side of the face (Bell's Palsy). With this type of lesion, the bilateral and contalateral inputs of the posterior and anterior routes, respectively, become irrelevant because the lesion is below the level of the medulla and the facial motor nucleus. Whereas at a level above the medulla a lesion occurring in one hemisphere would mean that the other hemisphere could still sufficiently innervate the posterior facial motor nucleus, a lesion affecting a lower motor neuron would eliminate innervation altogether because the nerves no longer have a means to receive compensatory contralateral input at a downstream decussation.

Thus, the main distinction between an UMN and LMN lesion is that in the former, there is hemiplegia of the contralateral mid- and lower-face, whereas in the latter, there is complete hemiplegia of the ipsilateral face.

Additional images

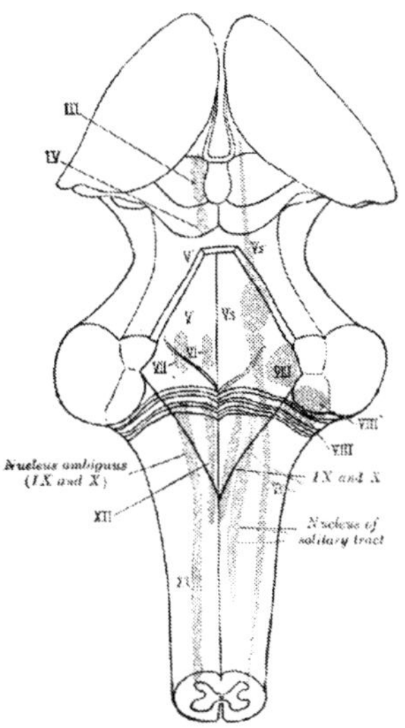

The cranial nerve nuclei schematically represented; dorsal view. Motor nuclei in red; sensory in blue.

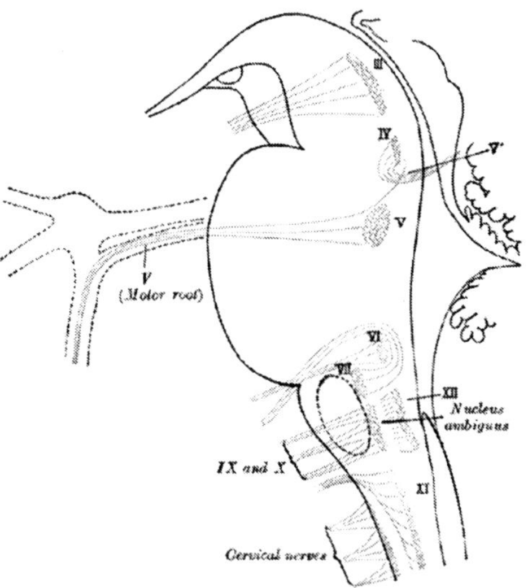

Nuclei of origin of cranial motor nerves schematically represented; lateral view.

Cochlear nuclei

Cochlear nuclei

Brain: Cochlear nuclei
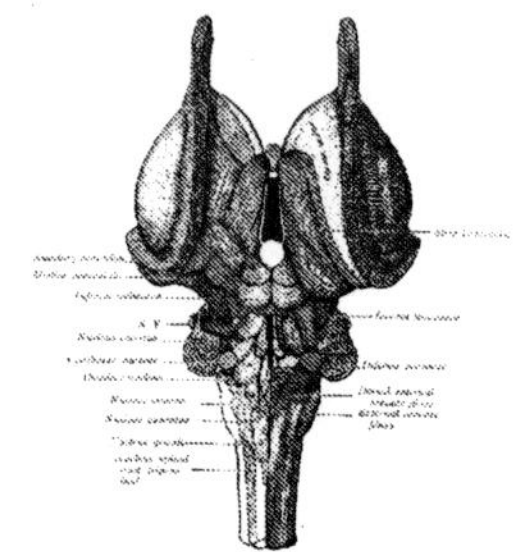
Dissection of brain-stem. Dorsal view. ("Cochlear nucleus" is labeled on left, fifth from the bottom.)
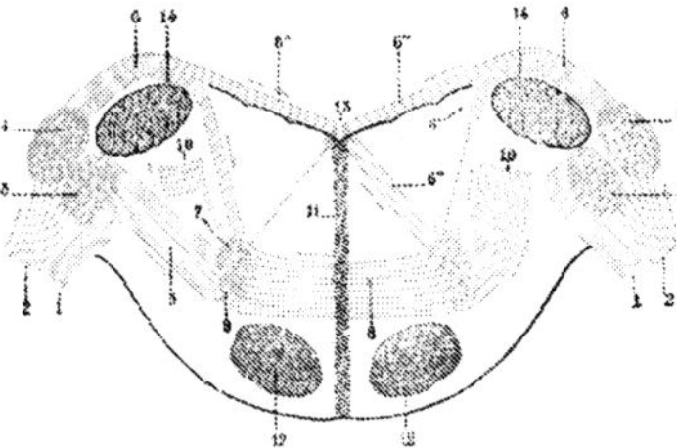

Terminal nuclei of the cochlear nerve, with their upper connections. (Schematic.) The vestibular nerve with its terminal nuclei and their efferent fibers have been suppressed. On the other hand, in order not to obscure the trapezoid body, the efferent fibers of the terminal nuclei on the right side have been resected in a considerable portion of their extent. The trapezoid body, therefore, shows only one-half of its fibers, viz., those that come from the left. 1. Vestibular nerve, divided at its entrance into the medulla oblongata. 2. Cochlear nerve. 3. Accessory nucleus of acoustic nerve. 4. Tuberculum acusticum. 5. Efferent fibers of accessory nucleus. 6. Efferent fibers of tuberculum acusticum, forming the striae medullares, with 6', their direct bundle going to the superior olivary nucleus of the same side; 6", their decussating bundles going to the superior olivary nucleus of the opposite side. 7. Superior olivary nucleus. 8. Trapezoid body. 9. Trapezoid nucleus. 10. Central acoustic tract (lateral lemniscus). 11. Raphé. 12. Cerebrospinal fasciculus. 13. Fourth ventricle. 14. Inferior peduncle.	
Latin	*nuclei cochleares*
Gray's	*subject #187 788* [1]
Part of	Medulla
System	Auditory system
Artery	AICA
NeuroNames	*hier-717* [2]

The **cochlear nuclei** (CN) consist of:

- (a) the **dorsal cochlear nucleus** (DCN), corresponding to the tuberculum acusticum on the dorso-lateral surface of the inferior peduncle; and
- (b) the **ventral** or **accessory cochlear nucleus**, placed between the two divisions of the nerve, on the ventral aspect of the inferior peduncle.

The ventral cochlear nucleus is further divided into the posteroventral cochlear nucleus (PVCN) and the anteroventral cochlear nucleus (AVCN).

The cochlear nucleus receives input from somatosensory parts of the brain.

Anatomy and function

The CN is the first relay station in the auditory system and is located at the dorso-lateral side of the brainstem, spanning the junction of the pons and medulla. Information is brought via the cochlear nerve, a part of Cranial nerve VIII (the vestibulocochlear nerve), to the CN. The cochlear nucleus can be divided into ventral and dorsal sections (DCN). The ventral part can further be divided into anterior and posterior sections (AVCN and PVCN), which are separated by the incoming auditory nerve fibers.

The auditory nerve fibers form a highly organized system of connections according to their peripheral innervation of the cochlea. Axons from the spiral ganglion cells of the lower frequency innervate the lateral-ventral portions of the dorsal cochlear nucleus and the ventrolateral portions of the anteroventral cochlear nucleus. In contrast, the axons from the higher frequency organ of corti hair cells project to the dorsal portion of the anteroventral cochlear nucleus and the dorsal-medial portions of the dorsal cochlear nucleus. The mid frequency projections end up in between the two extremes; in this way the frequency spectrum is preserved. The cochlear nuclei have long been thought to receive input only from the ipsilateral ear. There is evidence, however, for stimulation from the contralateral ear via the contralateral CN.

Just as the inner hair cells are arranged according to the best frequency (BF), so is the cochlear nucleus. This so-called tonotopic organization is preserved because only a few inner hair cells synapse on the dendrites of a nerve cell in the spiral ganglion, and the axon from that nerve cell synapes on only a very few dendrites in the cochlear nucleus.

The cochlear nucleus receives input from each spiral ganglion, but also receives input from *other* parts of the brain, such as auditory cortex, pontine nuclei, trigeminal ganglion and nucleus, dorsal column nuclei and the second dorsal root ganglion. The inputs from other areas of the brain play a role in sound localization.

Projections from the CN

There are three major projections from the cochlear nuclei. Through the medulla, one projection goes to the contralateral superior olivary complex (SOC) via the trapezoid body, whilst the other half shoots to the ipsilateral SOC. This projection is called the ventral acoustic stria (or, more commonly, the trapezoid body). Another projection, called the dorsal acoustic stria (DAS, also known as the stria of von Monakow), rises above the medulla into the pons where it hits the nucleus of the lateral lemniscus along with its kin, the intermediate acoustic stria (IAS, also known as the stria of Held). The IAS decussates across the medulla, before joining the ascending fibers in the contralateral lateral lemniscus. The lateral lemniscus contains cells of the nuclei of the lateral lemniscus, and in turn projects to the inferior colliculus. The inferior colliculus receives direct, monosynaptic projections from the superior olivary complex the contralateral dorsal acoustic stria, some classes of stellate neurons of the VCN, as well as from the different nuclei of the lateral lemniscus.

All of these inputs terminate in the inferior colliculus, although there are a few small projections that bypass the inferior colliculus and project to the medial geniculate, or other forebrain structures. The principal projection of the inferior colliculus is to the medial geniculate body in the thalamus. The medial geniculate then projects to the auditory cortex, in the superior temporal gyrus.

Cell types

There are four types of principal cells found in the cochlear nuclei: Bushy cells, stellate cells, octopus cells, and fusiform cells.

- *Bushy cells* are found in the anterior ventral cochlear nucleus (AVCN). These can be divided into spherical and globular bushy cells, depending on their appearance, and also their location. Within the AVCN here is an area of large spherical cells; caudal to this are smaller spherical cells, and globular cells. They have a few (1-4) very short dendrites with numerous small branching, which cause it to resemble a "bush". The bushy cells are only found in the ventral portion of the AVCN itself. The bushy cells have specialized electrical properties that allow them to transmit timing information from the auditory nerve to more central areas of the auditory system. Some bushy cells can even improve the precision of the timing information. Bushy cells have responses very similar to those in the auditory nerve. The primary difference is that spontaneous activity is decreased by stimulation by adjacent frequencies, therefore leading to an even sharper tuning curve than seen in auditory nerve cells. These cells are usually innervated only by a selected few axons, which dominate its firing patterns. These afferent axons wrap their terminal branches around the entire soma, creating a large synapse onto the bushy cells, which is named "Endbulb of Held". Therefore, a single unit recording of an electrically stimulated bushy neuron characteristically produces exactly one action potential and constitutes the primary response.
- *Stellate cells* (aka multipolar cells), morphologically, have a radial, star-like dendritic tree, which is where they get their name. They are also called chopper cells, in reference to their ability to fire a regularly-spaced train of action potentials for the duration of a tonal or noise stimulus. The chopping pattern is intrinsic to the electrical excitability of the stellate cell, and the firing rate depends on the strength of the auditory input more than on the frequency.
- *Octopus cells* are found in a small region of the Posterior Ventral Cochlear Nucleus (PVCN). The distinguishing features of these cells are their long, thick dendrites that typically emanate from one side of the cell body. Octopus cells produce an "Onset Response" to simple tonal stimuli. That is, they respond only at the onset of a specific frequency or frequency range at higher amplitudes. The octopus cells can fire with some of the highest temporal precision of any neuron in the brain. Electrical stimuli to the auditory nerve has been shown to evoke a graded post synaptic potential in the octopus cells. These EPSP's are very brief. The octopus cells are thought to be important extracting timing information. It has been reported that these cells can respond to click trains at a rate of 800 Hz.

- *Fusiform cells* (also known as *pyramidal cells*) are found in the Dorsal Cochlear Nucleus (DCN). See the separate page concerning the DCN.

Structures

The input of auditory stimulus is through the Auditory Nerve (CN VIII). The auditory stimulus further travels through the AVCN as neural impulses and branches through the following structures:

- Medial superior olive (MSO) via Trapezoid Body (TB) – Ipsilateral and contralateral stimulation for low frequency sounds.
- Lateral superior olive (LSO) directly and via TB – Ipsilateral stimulation for high frequency sounds.
- Medial Nucleus of Trapezoid body (MNTB) – Contralateral stimulation.
- Inferior colliculus – Contralateral stimulation.
- Neurotransmitters: There are four neurotransmitters responsible for transmission of neural impulses, namely, GABA, Norepinephrine, Glutamate, and Acetylcholine.
- Periolivary nuclei (PON) – Ipsilateral and Contralateral stimulation.
- Lateral lemniscus (LL) and Lemniscal Nuclei (LN) – Ipsilateral and Contralateral Stimulation.

See also

- Auditory system
- Cochlear nerve

References

Young, Eric D., Spirou, George A., Rice, John J., and Voigt, Herbert F., "Neural organization and responses to complex stimuli in the dorsal cochlear nucleus," Phil. Trans. R. Soc. Lond. B (1992) 336, 407-413 [3]

Additional images

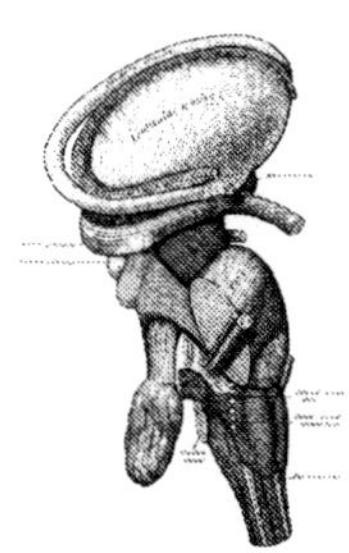

Dissection of brain-stem. Lateral view.

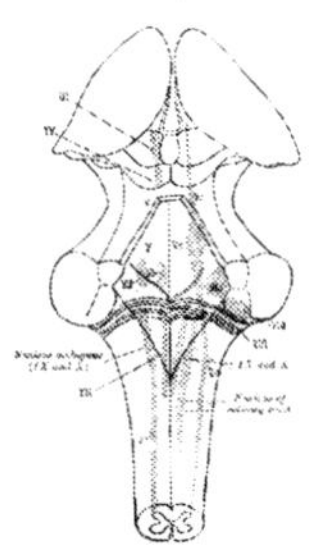

The cranial nerve nuclei schematically represented; dorsal view. Motor nuclei in red; sensory in blue.

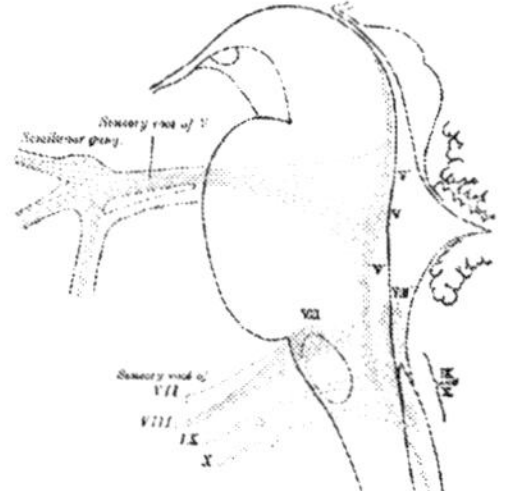

Primary terminal nuclei of the afferent (sensory) cranial nerves schematically represented; lateral view.

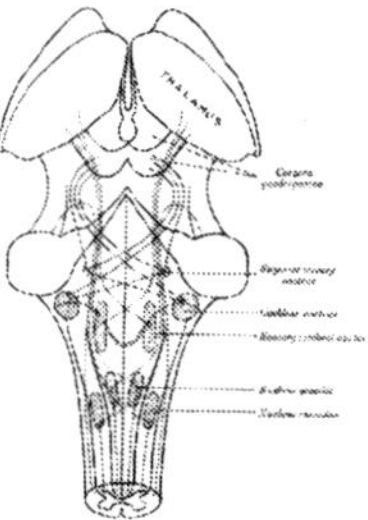

Scheme showing the course of the fibers of the lemniscus; medial lemniscus in blue, lateral in red.

External links

- University of Buffalo [1]
- Neuroanatomy at UW *Bs97/TEXT/P12/intro.htm* [2]
- Medical research council [3]
- Shore lab [4]

This article was originally based on an entry from a public domain edition of Gray's Anatomy. *As such, some of the information contained within it may be outdated.*

Dorsal cochlear nucleus

Dorsal cochlear nucleus

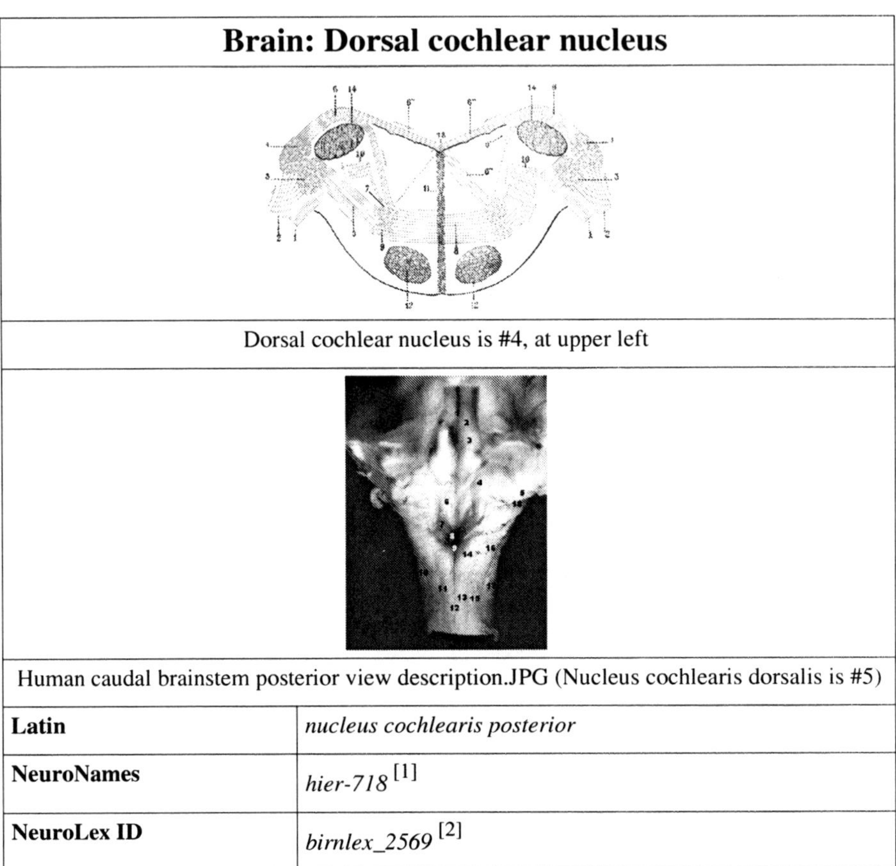

Brain: Dorsal cochlear nucleus	
Dorsal cochlear nucleus is #4, at upper left	
Human caudal brainstem posterior view description.JPG (Nucleus cochlearis dorsalis is #5)	
Latin	*nucleus cochlearis posterior*
NeuroNames	*hier-718* [1]
NeuroLex ID	*birnlex_2569* [2]

The **dorsal cochlear nucleus** (DCN, also known as the "tuberculum acousticum"), is a cortex-like structure on the dorso-lateral surface of the brainstem. Along with the ventral cochlear nucleus, it forms the cochlear nucleus, where all auditory nerve fibers from the cochlea form their first synapses.

Anatomy

The DCN differs from the ventral portion of the CN as it not only projects to the central nucleus of the Inferior Colliculus (ICC) but also receives efferent innervation from auditory cortex, superior olivary complex and inferior colliculus. The architecture and wiring of the DCN is similar to that of the cerebellum, a concept that currently is important in theories of DCN function. Thus, the DCN is thought to be involved with more complex auditory processing, rather than merely transferring information.

The fusiform (also called pyramidal) and giant cells are the principal cells of the DCN. There is no known physiological difference between these two cell types. These cells are the target of two different input systems. The first system arises from the auditory nerve, and carries acoustic information. The second set of inputs is relayed through a set of small cells called "granule" cells in the cochlear nucleus. The granule cells in turn are the target of a number of different inputs, including both those involved in auditory processing and, at least in lower mammals, somatosensory inputs associated with the head, the ear, and the jaw.

Projections from DCN principal cells form the dorsal acoustic stria, which ultimately terminate in the ICC. This projection overlaps with that of the LSO in a well defined manner, where they form the primary excitatory input for ICC type O units

Physiology

Principal cells in the DCN have very complex frequency intensity tuning curves. Classified as cochlear nucleus type IV cells, the firing rate may be very rapid in response to a low intensity sound at one frequency and then fall below the spontaneous rate with only a small increment in stimulus frequency or intensity. The firing rate may then increase with another increment in intensity or frequency. Type IV cells are excited by wide band noise, and particularly excited by a noise-notch stimulus directly below the cell's best frequency (BF).

While the VCN bushy cells aid in the location of a sound stimulus on the horizontal axis via their inputs to the superior olivary complex, type IV cells may participate in localization of the sound stimulus on the vertical axis. The pinna selectively amplifies frequencies, resulting in reduced sound energy at specific frequencies in certain regions of space. The complicated firing patterns of type IV cells makes them especially suited to detecting these notches, and with the combined power of these two localization systems, an ordinary person can locate where a firework explodes without the use of his eyes.

Somatosensory inputs inhibit type IV cell activity, possibly silencing their activity during head and pinna movements . While this has not been studied extensively, it may play an important role in sound source localization in elevation. A similar effect is seen in the visual system in an effect known as change blindness.

Current auditory models of the DCN employ a two-inhibitor model. Type IV cells receive excitation directly from the auditory nerve, and are inhibited by type II (vertical) cells and a wide band inhibitor (onset-c cells).

External links

- NIF Search - Dorsal Cochlear Nucleus [3] via the Neuroscience Information Framework

Vestibular nuclei

Vestibular nuclei

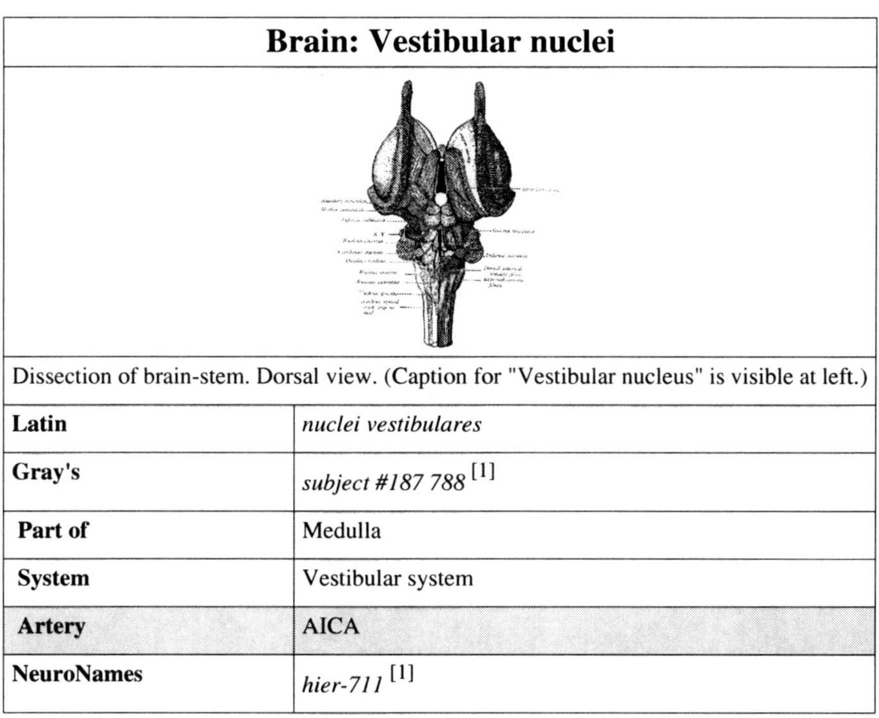

Brain: Vestibular nuclei	
Dissection of brain-stem. Dorsal view. (Caption for "Vestibular nucleus" is visible at left.)	
Latin	*nuclei vestibulares*
Gray's	*subject #187 788* [1]
Part of	Medulla
System	Vestibular system
Artery	AICA
NeuroNames	*hier-711* [1]

The **vestibular nuclei** are the cranial nuclei for the vestibular nerve.

In Terminologia Anatomica they are grouped in both the pons and medulla.

Subnuclei

There are 4 subnuclei; they are situated at the floor of the fourth ventricle.

Name	Location	Notes
medial vestibular nucleus (dorsal or chief vestibular nucleus)	medulla (floor of fourth ventricle)	corresponding to the lower part of the area acustica in the rhomboid fossa; the caudal end of this nucleus is sometimes termed the **descending** or **spinal vestibular nucleus**.
lateral vestibular nucleus or nucleus of Deiters	medulla (upper)	consisting of large cells and situated in the lateral angle of the rhomboid fossa; the dorso-lateral part of this nucleus is sometimes termed the **nucleus of Bechterew**.
inferior vestibular nucleus	medulla (lower)	
superior vestibular nucleus	pons	

Path from medial and lateral nuclei

The fibers of the vestibular nerve enter the medulla oblongata on the medial side of those of the cochlear, and pass between the inferior peduncle and the spinal tract of the trigeminal.

They then divide into ascending and descending fibers. The latter end by arborizing around the cells of the medial nucleus, which is situated in the area acustica of the rhomboid fossa. The ascending fibers either end in the same manner or in the lateral nucleus, which is situated lateral to the area acustica and farther from the ventricular floor.

Some of the axons of the cells of the lateral nucleus, and possibly also of the medial nucleus, are continued upward through the inferior peduncle to the roof nuclei of the opposite side of the cerebellum, to which also other fibers of the vestibular root are prolonged without interruption in the nuclei of the medulla oblongata.

A second set of fibres from the medial and lateral nuclei end partly in the tegmentum, while the remainder ascend in the medial longitudinal fasciculus to arborize around the cells of the nuclei of the oculomotor nerve.

Fibres from the lateral vestibular nucleus also pass via the vestibulospinal tract, to anterior horn cells at many levels in the spinal cord, in order to co-ordinate head and trunk movements.

See also

- Vestibular nerve

Additional images

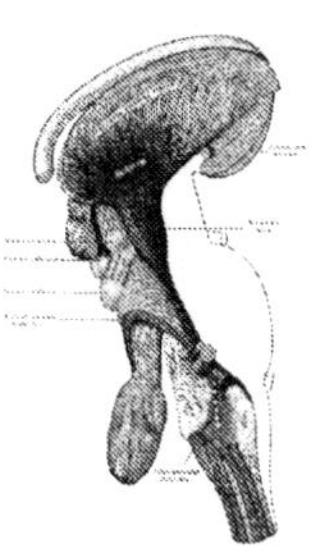

Deep dissection of brain-stem. Lateral view.

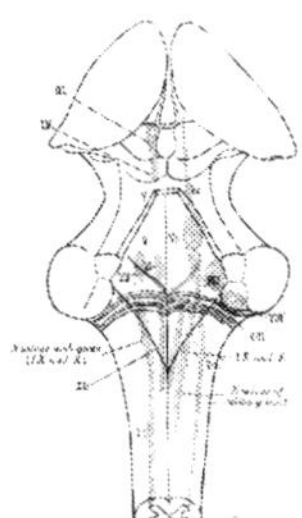

The cranial nerve nuclei schematically represented; dorsal view. Motor nuclei in red; sensory in blue.

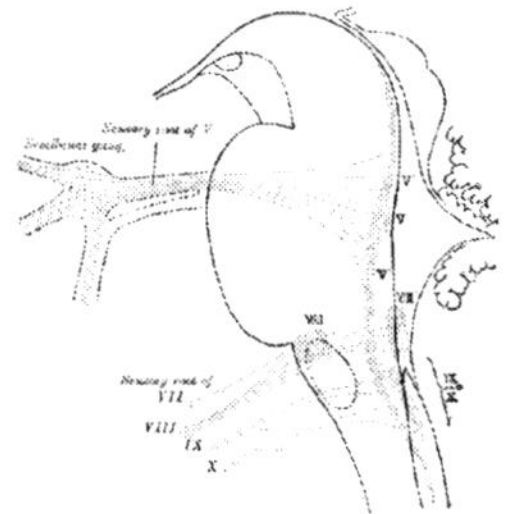

Primary terminal nuclei of the afferent (sensory) cranial nerves schematically represented; lateral view.

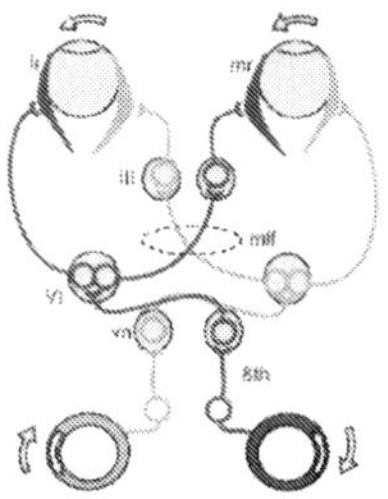

Vestibulo-ocular reflex

External links

- Neuroanatomy at UW *Bs97/TEXT/P13/intro.htm* [2]
- http://www.lib.mcg.edu/edu/eshuphysio/program/section8/8ch6/s8ch6_29.htm
- Parkinson.org [3]

This article was originally based on an entry from a public domain edition of Gray's Anatomy. *As such, some of the information contained within it may be outdated.*

Spinal trigeminal nucleus

Spinal trigeminal nucleus

Brain: Spinal trigeminal nucleus	
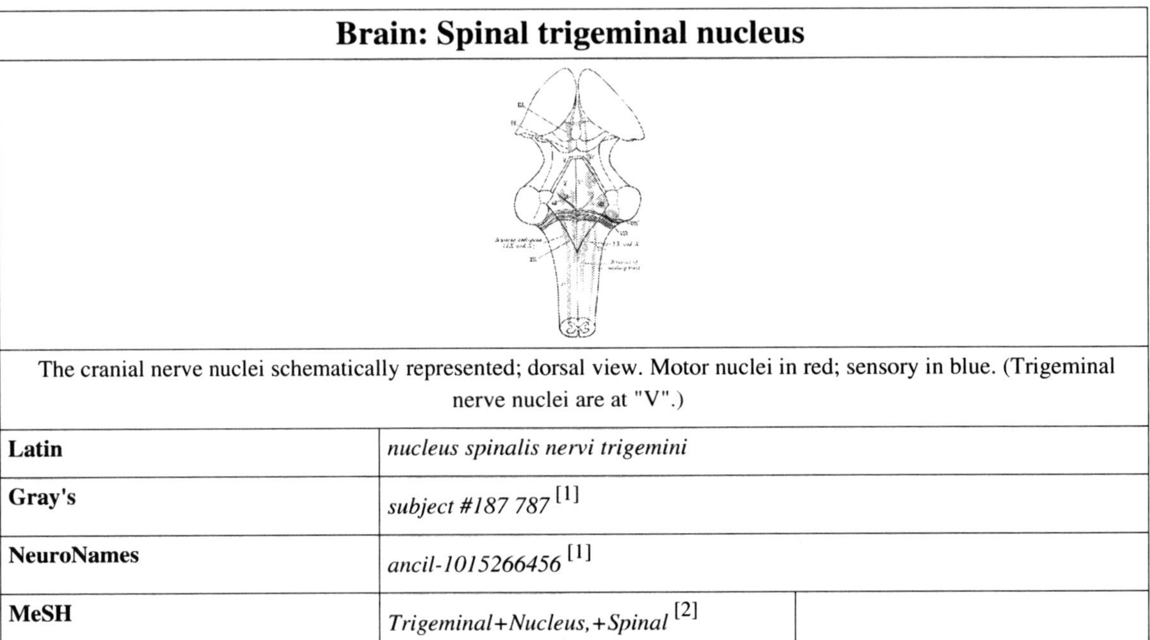	
The cranial nerve nuclei schematically represented; dorsal view. Motor nuclei in red; sensory in blue. (Trigeminal nerve nuclei are at "V".)	
Latin	*nucleus spinalis nervi trigemini*
Gray's	*subject #187 787* [1]
NeuroNames	*ancil-1015266456* [1]
MeSH	*Trigeminal+Nucleus,+Spinal* [2]

The **spinal trigeminal nucleus** is a nucleus in the medulla that receives information about deep/crude touch, pain, and temperature from the ipsilateral face. The facial, glossopharyngeal, and vagus nerves also convey pain information from their areas to the spinal trigeminal nucleus.

See also

Trigeminal nerve nuclei

Spinal accessory nucleus

Spinal accessory nucleus

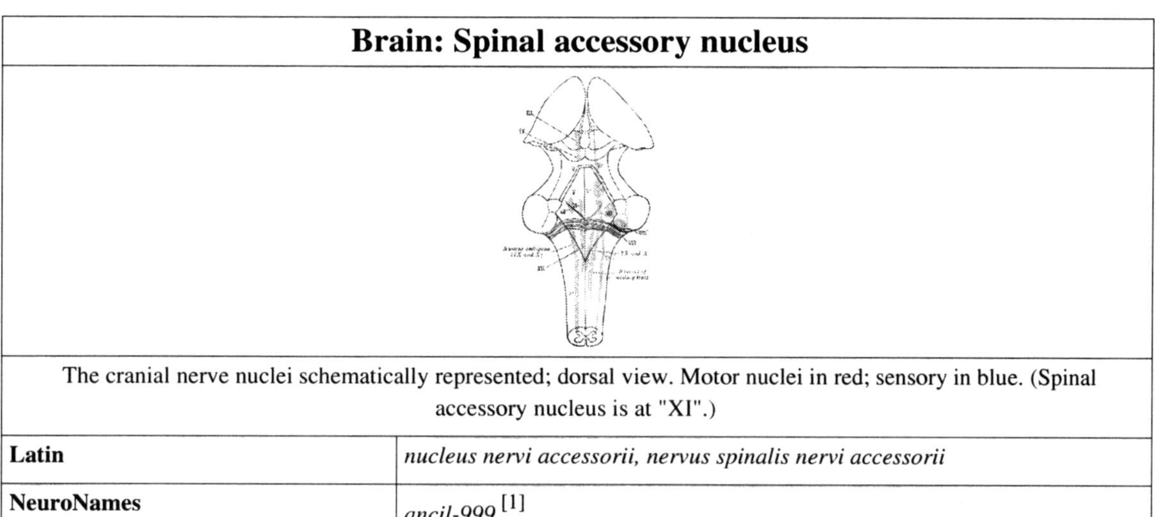

Brain: Spinal accessory nucleus	
The cranial nerve nuclei schematically represented; dorsal view. Motor nuclei in red; sensory in blue. (Spinal accessory nucleus is at "XI".)	
Latin	*nucleus nervi accessorii, nervus spinalis nervi accessorii*
NeuroNames	*ancil-999* [1]

The spinal accessory nucleus lies within the cervical spinal cord (C1-C5) in the ventral horn. The nucleus ambiguus is classically said to provide the "cranial component" of the accessory nerve.

However, the very existence of this cranial component has been recently questioned and seen as contributing exclusively to the vagus nerve.

The terminology continues to be used in describing both human anatomy, and that of other animals.

Additional images

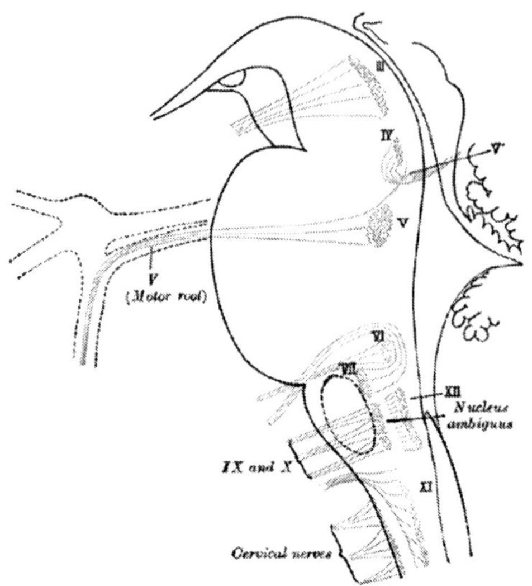

Nuclei of origin of cranial motor nerves schematically represented; lateral view.

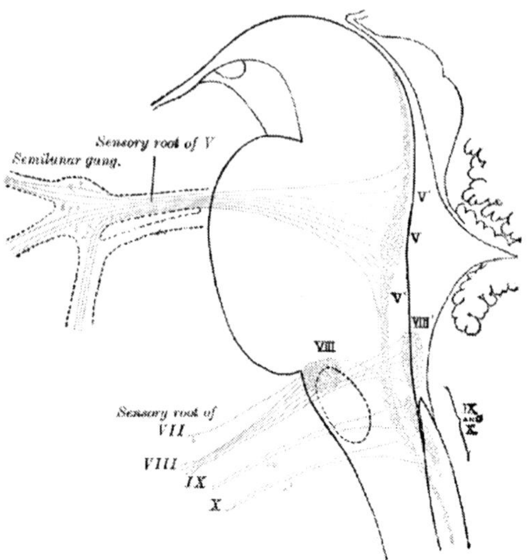

Primary terminal nuclei of the afferent (sensory) cranial nerves schematically represented; lateral view.

External links

- Sylvius [2]
- University of New Mexico [3]
- Georgetown [4]

Internal arcuate fibers

Internal arcuate fibers

Internal arcuate fibers	
Diagram showing the course of the arcuate fibers. (Testut.) 1. Medulla oblongata anterior surface. 2. Anterior median fissure. 3. Fourth ventricle. 4. Inferior olivary nucleus, with the accessory olivary nuclei. 5. Gracile nucleus. 6. Cuneate nucleus. 7. Trigeminal. 8. Inferior peduncles, seen from in front. 9. Posterior external arcuate fibers. 10. Anterior external arcuate fibers. 11. Internal arcuate fibers. 12. Peduncle of inferior olivary nucleus. 13. Nucleus arcuatus. 14. Vagus. 15. Hypoglossal.	
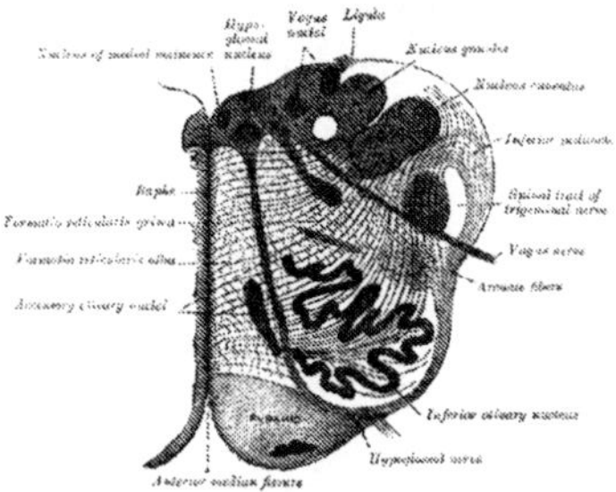	
Section of the medulla oblongata at about the middle of the olive. (Arcuate fibers labeled at center right.)	
Latin	*fibrae arcuatae internae*
Gray's	*subject #187 782* [1]

Internal arcuate fibers are the axons of second-order neurons contained within the gracile and cuneate nuclei of the medulla oblongata.

These fibers cross (decussate) from one side of the medulla to the other to form the medial lemniscus.

Part of the dorsal column-medial lemniscus system (second neuron), the internal arcuate fibers are important for relaying the sensation of fine touch and proprioception to the thalamus and ultimately to the cerebral cortex.

External links

- NeuroNames *Hier-792* [2]
- Photo [3] at Indiana.edu

Dorsal column nuclei

Dorsal column nuclei

Dorsal column nuclei	
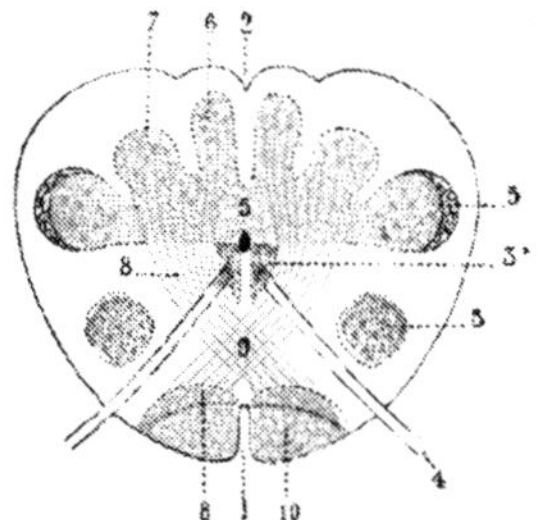	
Present at the junction between the spinal cord and medulla oblongata, the dorsal column nuclei consist of paired gracile and cuneate nuclei (labels 6 and 7, respectively).	
System	Somatosensory system

In neuroanatomy, the **dorsal column nuclei** are a pair of nuclei in the brainstem. The name refers collectively to the cuneate nucleus and gracile nucleus, which are present at the junction between the spinal cord and the medulla oblongata. Both nuclei contain secondary neurons of the dorsal column-medial lemniscus pathway, which carries fine touch and proprioceptive information from the body to the brain.

The gracile nucleus is medial to the cuneate nucleus; its neurons receive afferent input from dorsal root ganglion sensory neurons subserving the lower trunk and limbs, while neurons of the cuneate nucleus receive connections from dorsal root neurons innervating the upper body. Neurons of the dorsal column nuclei send axons that form the internal arcuate fibers, decussating (crossing to the opposite side) to form the medial lemniscus, ultimately synapsing with third-order neurons of the thalamus.

Because each nucleus contains a large population of neurons, the dorsal column nuclei give rise to characteristic bumps or *tubercles* when viewing the posterior side of the intact brainstem. In particular, the cuneate nucleus gives rise to the cuneate tubercle, while the gracile nucleus gives rise to the gracile tubercle.

Prethalamus

Prethalamus

The ***prethalamus*** (formerly described as *ventral thalamus*) or subthalamus is part of the diencephalon and therefore part of the brain.

Developmental biologist prefer the term prethalamus, as it can be genetically defined (Puelles and Rubenstein, 2003), whereas (human) anatomists often use the expression subthalamus.

The prethalamus is part of the mid-diencephalic territory (MDT) containing also the zona limitans intrathalamica (ZLI), and the thalamus. Caudally, the prethalamus is separated from the thalamus by the ZLI acting as lineage restriction boundary. The pro-neural gene Dlx2 serves a typical marker of the prethalamus. Typical nuclei of the prethalamus are the zona incerta, thalamic reticular nucleus, and the fields of Forel.

The prethalamus is patterned by Sonic hedgehog signalling from the ZLI. Anatomically, it develops efferent (output) connections to the striatum (caudate nucleus and putamen) in the telencephalon, to the thalamus (medial and lateral nuclear groups) in the diencephalon, and to the red nucleus and substantia nigra in the mesencephalon. It receives afferent (input) connections from the substantia nigra and striatum.

Pyramid (brainstem)

Pyramid (brainstem)

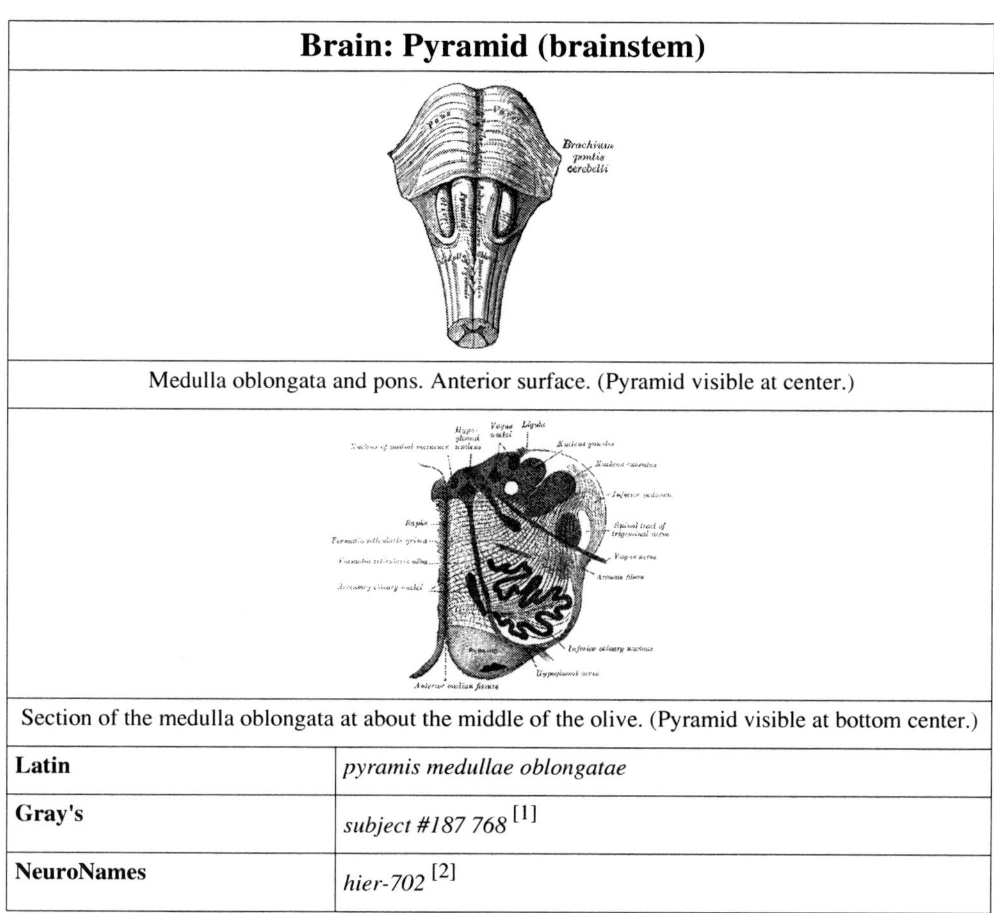

Brain: Pyramid (brainstem)	
Medulla oblongata and pons. Anterior surface. (Pyramid visible at center.)	
Section of the medulla oblongata at about the middle of the olive. (Pyramid visible at bottom center.)	
Latin	*pyramis medullae oblongatae*
Gray's	*subject #187 768* [1]
NeuroNames	*hier-702* [2]

The anterior or ventral portion of the medulla oblongata is named the **pyramid** and lies between the anterior median fissure and the antero-lateral sulcus.

Its upper end is slightly constricted, and between it and the pons the fibers of the abducent nerve emerge; a little below the pons it becomes enlarged and prominent, and finally tapers into the anterior funiculus of the medulla spinalis, with which, at first sight, it appears to be directly continuous.

See also

- Corticospinal tract (also known as "pyramidal tract")
- Decussation of the pyramids

Additional images

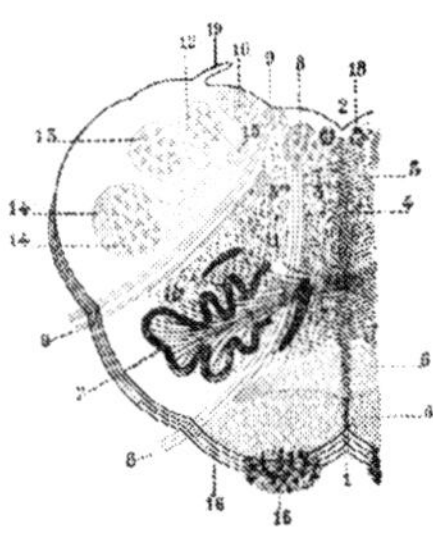

The formatio reticularis of the medulla oblongata, shown by a transverse section passing through the middle of the olive.

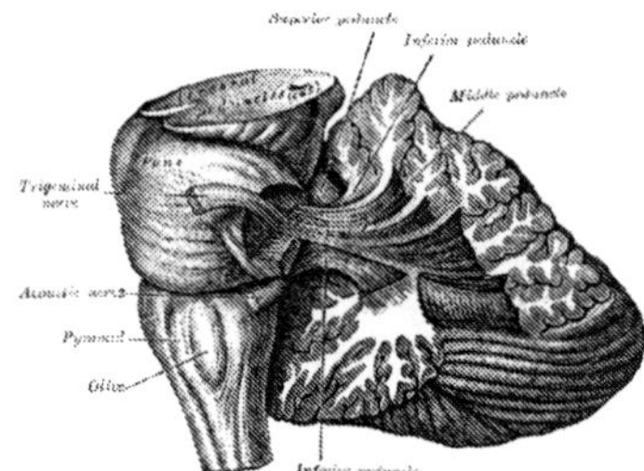

Dissection showing the projection fibers of the cerebellum.

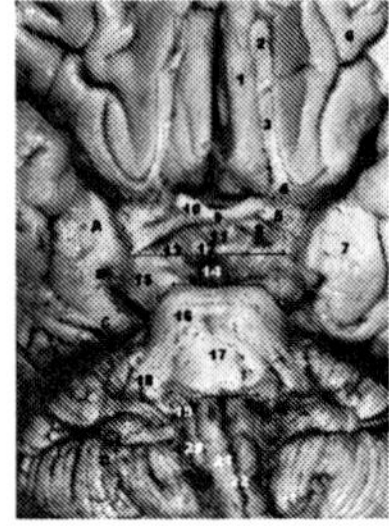

Human brainstem anterior view

External links

- *pyramid+of+medulla+oblongata* [3] at eMedicine Dictionary
- Diagram at csus.edu [4]

This article was originally based on an entry from a public domain edition of Gray's Anatomy. *As such, some of the information contained within it may be outdated.*

Cerebral crus

Cerebral crus

Brain: Cerebral crus	
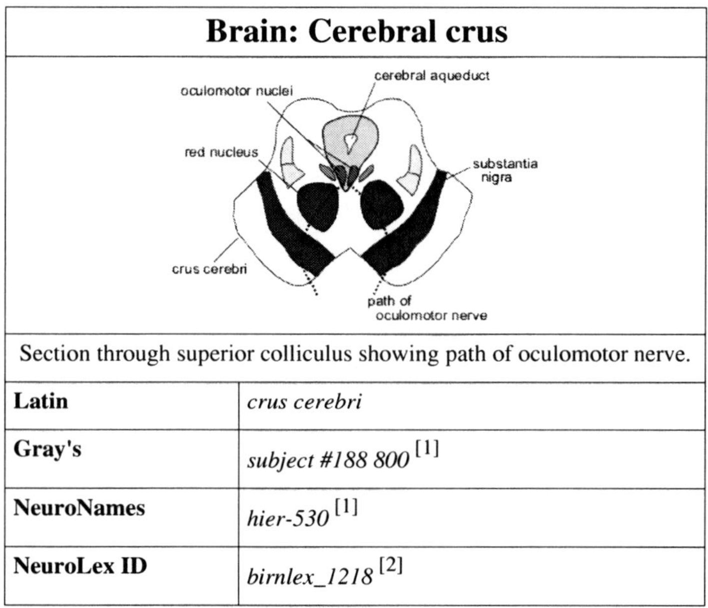	
Section through superior colliculus showing path of oculomotor nerve.	
Latin	*crus cerebri*
Gray's	*subject #188 800* [1]
NeuroNames	*hier-530* [1]
NeuroLex ID	*birnlex_1218* [2]

The **cerebral crus** is the anterior portion of the cerebral peduncle which contains the motor tracts, the plural of which is **cerebral crura**.

In some older texts, it is used as a synonym for the entire cerebral peduncle, not just the anterior portion of it.

Additional images

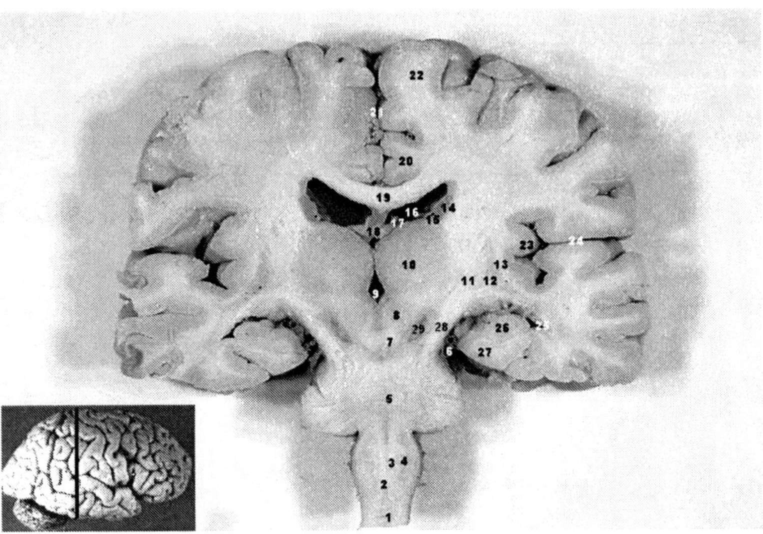

Human brain frontal (coronal) section

External links

- Atlas of anatomy at UMich *n2a2p1* [3]
- Atlas of anatomy at UMich *n1a5p3* [4]
- NIF Search - Cerebral Crus [5] via the Neuroscience Information Framework

This article was originally based on an entry from a public domain edition of Gray's Anatomy. *As such, some of the information contained within it may be outdated.*

Anterolateral sulcus of medulla

Anterolateral sulcus of medulla

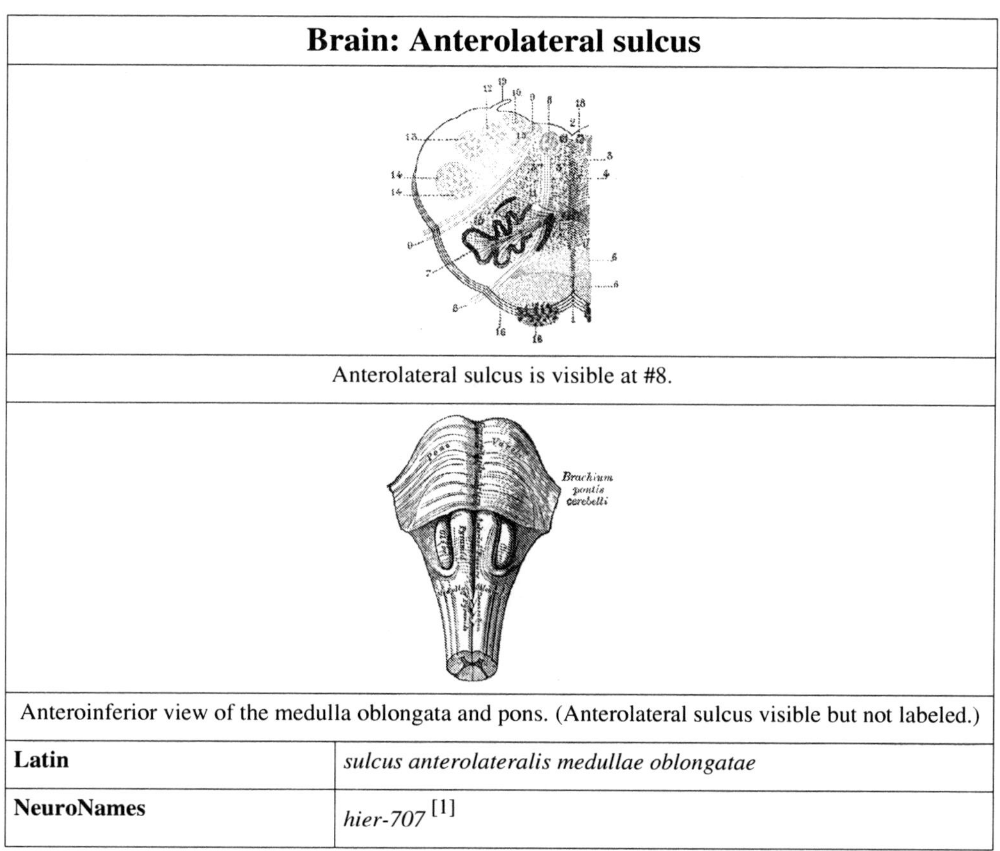

Brain: Anterolateral sulcus	
Anterolateral sulcus is visible at #8.	
Anteroinferior view of the medulla oblongata and pons. (Anterolateral sulcus visible but not labeled.)	
Latin	*sulcus anterolateralis medullae oblongatae*
NeuroNames	*hier-707* [1]

The **anterolateral sulcus** (or **ventrolateral sulcus**) is a sulcus on the side of the medulla oblongata. The rootlets of cranial nerve XII (the hypoglossal nerve) emerge from this sulcus.

See also

- Anterolateral sulcus of spinal cord

External links

- http://www.ib.amwaw.edu.pl/anatomy/atlas/image_02e.htm

Thalamic fasciculus

Thalamic fasciculus

Brain: Thalamic fasciculus

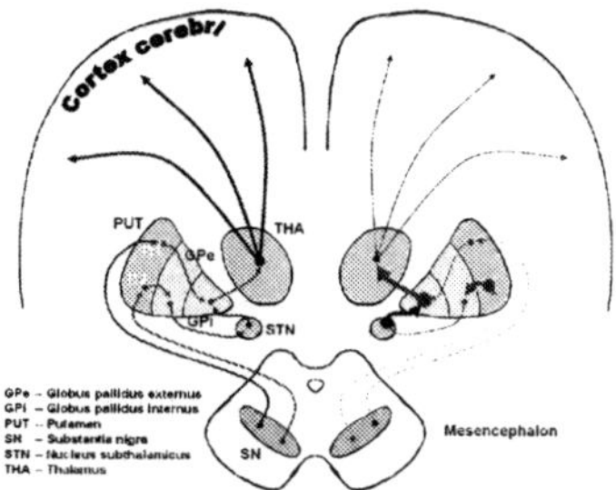

The image shows dopaminergic pathways of the human brain in normal condition (left) and Parkinsons Disease (right). Red Arrows indicate suppression of the target, blue arrows indicate stimulation of target structure. (Thalamic fasciculus visible but not labeled, as red line from GPi to THA.)

Latin	*fasciculus thalamicus*
NeuroNames	*hier-422* [1]

The **thalamic fasciculus** is a component of the subthalamus. It is sometimes considered synonymous with "field H1 of Forel". Nerve fibres forming a composite bundle containing cerebellothalamic (crossed) and pallidothalamic (uncrossed) fibres that is insinuated between the thalamus and zona incerta.

The thalamic fasciculus consists of the joint fibers of the ansa lenticularis and the lenticular fasciculus, coming from different portions of the medial globus pallidus, before they jointly enter the ventral lateral nucleus of the thalamus.

External links

- http://www.meddean.luc.edu/lumen/MedEd/Neuro/frames/nlDEs/nl06fr.htm
- http://www.endotext.org/neuroendo/neuroendo3b/neuroendo3b_2.htm (see figure #12)
- http://isc.temple.edu/neuroanatomy/lab/atlas/mdbg/

Lenticular fasciculus

Lenticular fasciculus

<table>
<tr><th colspan="2">Brain: Lenticular fasciculus</th></tr>
<tr><td colspan="2">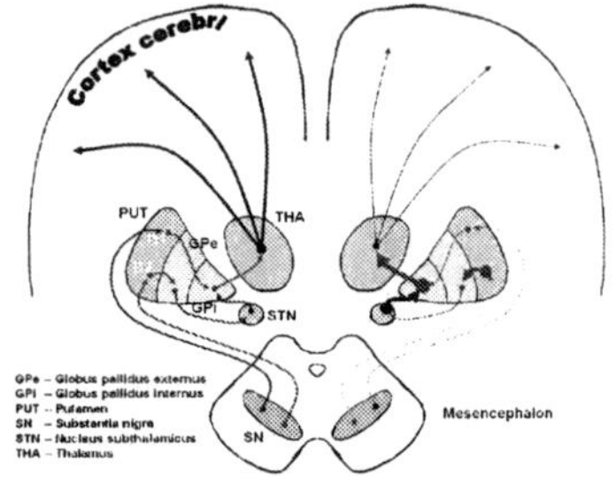
</td></tr>
<tr><td colspan="2">The image shows dopaminergic pathways of the human brain in normal condition (left) and Parkinsons Disease (right). Red Arrows indicate suppression of the target, blue arrows indicate stimulation of target structure. (Lenticular fasciculus visible but not labeled, as red line from GPi to THA.)</td></tr>
<tr><td>Latin</td><td>fasciculus lenticularis</td></tr>
<tr><td>NeuroNames</td><td>hier-424 [1]</td></tr>
</table>

The **lenticular fasciculus** is a tract connecting the globus pallidus to the Thalamic fasciculus. The thalamic fasciculus (composed of the lenticular fasciculus and ansa lenticularis) runs into the Thalamus. It is sometimes considered synonymous with "field H2 of Forel".

It connects the globus pallidus to the thalamus.

External links

- http://www.endotext.org/neuroendo/neuroendo3b/neuroendo3b_2.htm (see figure #12)
- http://isc.temple.edu/neuroanatomy/lab/atlas/mdbg/

Anterior cochlear nucleus

Anterior cochlear nucleus

Brain: Anterior cochlear nucleus	
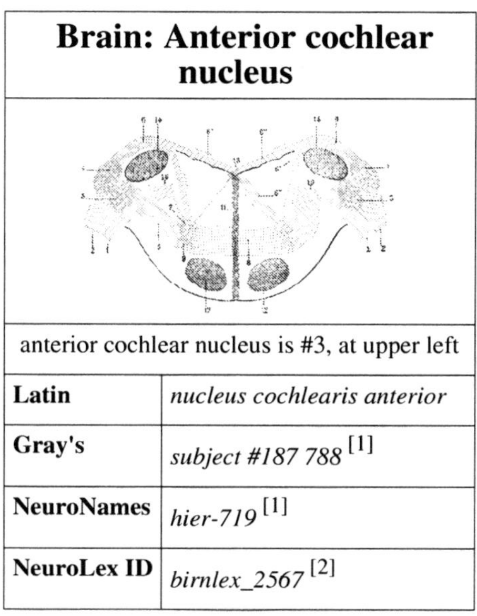	
anterior cochlear nucleus is #3, at upper left	
Latin	*nucleus cochlearis anterior*
Gray's	*subject #187 788* [1]
NeuroNames	*hier-719* [1]
NeuroLex ID	*birnlex_2567* [2]

The **ventral cochlear nucleus** (or **anterior**, or **accessory**), placed between the two divisions of the cochlear nerve, is on the ventral aspect of the inferior peduncle. Composed of several regions of distinct cell types, this nucleus serves primarily as a relay station for ascending auditory information. Bushy cells in the anterior ventral cochlear nucleus (AVCN), which receive end bulbs of held from auditory nerve fibers, project to the superior olivary complex through the trapezoid body and intermediate acoustic stria. Other cell types project to the lateral lemniscus and the inferior colliculus directly.

Cell types

The VCN contains several cell types, which correspond fairly well with different physiological unit types. Additionally, these cell types generally have specific projection patterns.

Bushy Cells

Named due to the branching, tree-like, nature of their dentritic fields, visible using Golgi's method, receive large end bulbs of held from auditory nerve fibers. These cells can be further subdivided into spherical and globular types based upon their appearance in Nissl-stained material, and their location in the nucleus (anterior AVCN and posterior AVCN respectively).

Globular

Globular bushy cells project large axons to the contralateral MNTB where they synapse onto principal cells via a single calyx of held, and several smaller collaterals synapse ipsilaterally in the posterior (PPO) & dorsolateral periolivary (DLPO) nuclei, lateral superior olive (LSO), and lateral nucleus of the trapezoid body (LNTB); contralaterally in the dorsomedial periolivary nucleus (DMPO), ventral nucleus of the trapezoid body (VNTB), nucleus paragigantocellularis lateralis (PGL), and Ventral nucleus of the lateral lemniscus (VNLL). Axons always send a collateral into the MNTB, but do not necessarily give rise to collaterals that innervate each of the other nuclei.

Spherical

Spherical bushy cells project ipsilaterally to the LSO, bilaterally to the Medial superior olive (MSO) and LNTB, and contralaterally to the VNTB and VNLL. The most important purpose of these projections seems to be to imbue the MSO and LSO with their interaural time and level sensitivities (respectively).

Octopus cells

- Needs information added

Multipolar (Stellate) cells

- Needs information added

Anterior Ventral Cochlear Nucleus (AVCN)

- The AVCN can be subdivided based upon the cytoarchitecture of the region.
  - Typical subdivisions are defined as: Anterior (AAVCN), Posterior(PAVCN), Posterodorsal (PDAVCN), and posteroventral (PVAVCN).

- A well defined tonotopy is evident. Lateral PVAVCN, Medial PVAVCN, and medial PDAVCN roughly correspond to the low (<1 kHz), middle (4-8 kHz), and high (>16 kHz) frequency regions defined by Bourk.
- The AVCN projects to nearly all brainstem auditory structures. High frequency regions tend to project to contralaterally, and low frequency regions bilaterally, preserving the tonotopic organization of the ascending auditory pathway.
- Stellate/multipolar cells form the projection to both inferior colliculi (central nucleus and dorsal cortex), and synapse in a banded pattern, following the tonotopy of the region.

Posterior Ventral Cochlear Nucleus (PVCN)

- Needs information added

References

This article was originally based on an entry from a public domain edition of Gray's Anatomy. *As such, some of the information contained within it may be outdated.*

Pallidothalamic tracts

Pallidothalamic tracts

Brain: Pallidothalamic tracts
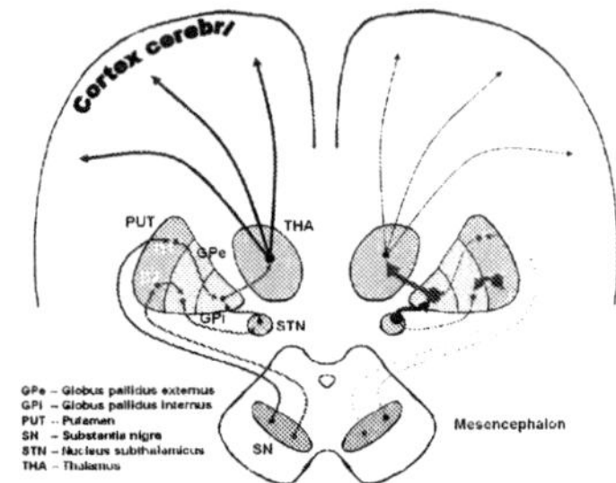
The image shows dopaminergic pathways of the human brain in normal condition (left) and Parkinsons Disease (right). Red Arrows indicate suppression of the target, blue arrows indicate stimulation of target structure. (Pallidothalamic connections visible but not labeled, as red line from GPi to THA.)

The **pallidothalamic connections** (or **pallidothalamic tracts**) are a part of the basal ganglia. They provide connectivity between the globus pallidus and the thalamus, primarily the ventral anterior nucleus and the ventral lateral nucleus.

Anatomy

It is composed of the Ansa lenticularis, the Lenticular fasciculus (Forel's Field H2), and Thalamic fasciculus (Forel's Field H1).

- The **ansa lenticularis** is composed of fibers that pass from the ventral aspect of the globus pallidus and sweep around the posterior limb of the internal capsule. They connect with the fibers of the **lenticular fasciculus** in the **Field of Forel (H)** to form the thalamic fasciculus.
- The **lenticular fasciculus** (also known as **Forel's Field H2**) is composed of fibers that pass from the internal part of the globus pallidus, *through* the posterior limb of the internal capsule, around the zona incerta. These fibers connect with the fibers of the **ansa lenticularis** in the **Field of Forel (H)** to form the thalamic fasciculus.
- The **thalamic fasciculus** (also known as **Forel's Field H1**) is formed by the fibers of the **ansa lenticularis** and the **lenticular fasciculus** that merge in the **Field of Forel (H)**. The fibers of this fasciculus then travel to the thalamus and primarily terminate in the ventral anterior nucleus and

ventral lateral nucleus. Some fibers travel to the interthalamic nuclei.

Pontine micturition center

Pontine micturition center

The **Pontine micturition center** (PMC, also known as **Barrington's Nucleus**) is a collection of cell bodies located in the rostral pons in the brainstem that is involved in the supraspinal regulation of micturition (urination). The PMC makes connections with other brain centers to control micturition, including the hypothalamus, the cerebral cortex and periaqueductal gray (PAG). The PAG in particular acts a relay station for ascending and descending bladder information from the spinal cord.

Regulation

In humans, neurons in the PMC send descending projections to Onuf's nucleus and to the parasympathetic nucleus in the spinal cord while receiving ascending input from the level of the sacral and lumbar cord. During bladder filling, neurons within the PMC are turned off, but at a critical level of bladder distention, the afferent activity arising from mechanoreceptors in the bladder wall switches the PMC on and enhances its activity. This activation results in relaxation of the urethra and contraction of the bladder due to concomitant stimulation of parasympathetic and inhibition of sympathetic outflow to the bladder, as well as removal of somatic activation of the external urethral sphincter.

References

- Fowler CJ, Griffiths D, de Groat WC. (June 9, 2008) "The neural control of micturition." *Nature Reviews: Neuroscience* (6):453-66
- Kuipers R, Mouton LJ, Holstege G. (January 1, 2006) "Afferent projections to the pontine micturition center in the cat." *The Journal of Comparative Neurology* 494(1):36-53
- Sasaki M. (December 5, 2005) "Role of Barrington's nucleus in micturition". *The Journal of Comparative Neurology* 5;493(1):21-6

Fields of forel

Fields of forel

Fields of Forel is an area in a deep part of the brain known as the diencephalon. It is below the thalamus and consists of three defined, white matter areas of the subthalamus. These three regions are named "H fields" (for Haubenfelder). The first, field H1, is the thalamic fasciculus, a horizontal white matter tract between the subthalamus and the thalamus. These fibers are projections to the thalamus from the basal ganglia (globus pallidus) and the cerebellum. H1 is separated from H2 by the zona incerta. Field H2 is also made up of projections from the pallidum to the thalamus, but these course the subthalamic nucleus (dorsal). Field H3 (aka the prerubral field), is a large zone of mixed gray and white matter located just rostral (In front) of the red nucleus.

External links

1. http://www.biology-online.org/dictionary/Fields_of_forel 2. Forel, A. (1877). "Untersuchungen über die Haubenregion und ihre oberen Verknüpfungen im Gehirne des Menschen und einiger Säugethiere, mit Beiträgen zu den Methoden der Gehirnuntersuchung". Archiv für Psychiatrie und Nervenkrankheiten 7: 393–495. doi:10.1007/BF02041873.

Article Sources and Contributors

Medulla oblongata *Source*: http://en.wikipedia.org/?oldid=389455114 *Contributors*: 1 anonymous edits

Pons *Source*: http://en.wikipedia.org/?oldid=388577916 *Contributors*: 1 anonymous edits

Brainstem *Source*: http://en.wikipedia.org/?oldid=390027937 *Contributors*: Ksanyi

List of regions in the human brain *Source*: http://en.wikipedia.org/?oldid=390125919 *Contributors*: John of Reading

Midbrain *Source*: http://en.wikipedia.org/?oldid=385915469 *Contributors*: Vojtech.dostal

Medial lemniscus *Source*: http://en.wikipedia.org/?oldid=384222122 *Contributors*: Eleassar

Nucleus ambiguus *Source*: http://en.wikipedia.org/?oldid=387707543 *Contributors*: Uwe Gille

Medial longitudinal fasciculus *Source*: http://en.wikipedia.org/?oldid=380773165 *Contributors*: Eleassar

Lateral lemniscus *Source*: http://en.wikipedia.org/?oldid=327592025 *Contributors*: ZooFari

Locus coeruleus *Source*: http://en.wikipedia.org/?oldid=385745571 *Contributors*: Hmains

Fourth ventricle *Source*: http://en.wikipedia.org/?oldid=389673698 *Contributors*: 1 anonymous edits

Cuneate nucleus *Source*: http://en.wikipedia.org/?oldid=380976086 *Contributors*: Eleassar

Superior colliculus *Source*: http://en.wikipedia.org/?oldid=389300105 *Contributors*: Anthonyhcole

Inferior colliculus *Source*: http://en.wikipedia.org/?oldid=373010299 *Contributors*: Josh Jorgensen

Midbrain tectum *Source*: http://en.wikipedia.org/?oldid=351948510 *Contributors*: Woohookitty

Periaqueductal gray *Source*: http://en.wikipedia.org/?oldid=382936544 *Contributors*: Tryptofish

Olivary body *Source*: http://en.wikipedia.org/?oldid=324518034 *Contributors*: Arcadian

Thalamic reticular nucleus *Source*: http://en.wikipedia.org/?oldid=378542248 *Contributors*: Anthonyhcole

Abducens nucleus *Source*: http://en.wikipedia.org/?oldid=371361227 *Contributors*: Uwe Gille

Pontine nuclei *Source*: http://en.wikipedia.org/?oldid=349589306 *Contributors*: Anthonyhcole

Rhombencephalon *Source*: http://en.wikipedia.org/?oldid=366878848 *Contributors*: Bgpaulus

Metencephalon *Source*: http://en.wikipedia.org/?oldid=332225009 *Contributors*:

Climbing fiber *Source*: http://en.wikipedia.org/?oldid=385760384 *Contributors*:

Apneustic respirations *Source*: http://en.wikipedia.org/?oldid=266433821 *Contributors*: 1 anonymous edits

Corpora quadrigemina *Source*: http://en.wikipedia.org/?oldid=384771602 *Contributors*:

Accessory cuneate nucleus *Source*: http://en.wikipedia.org/?oldid=332416111 *Contributors*: Arcadian

Zona incerta *Source*: http://en.wikipedia.org/?oldid=387953511 *Contributors*: LilHelpa

Obex *Source*: http://en.wikipedia.org/?oldid=342246740 *Contributors*: 1 anonymous edits

Paramedian pontine reticular formation *Source*: http://en.wikipedia.org/?oldid=356678746 *Contributors*: Cathy8630

Facial motor nucleus *Source*: http://en.wikipedia.org/?oldid=384997316 *Contributors*: Jabaway

Cochlear nuclei *Source*: http://en.wikipedia.org/?oldid=375196286 *Contributors*: 1 anonymous edits

Dorsal cochlear nucleus *Source*: http://en.wikipedia.org/?oldid=366176008 *Contributors*:

Vestibular nuclei *Source*: http://en.wikipedia.org/?oldid=363719685 *Contributors*: Captain-n00dle

Spinal trigeminal nucleus *Source*: http://en.wikipedia.org/?oldid=380781850 *Contributors*: Eleassar

Spinal accessory nucleus *Source*: http://en.wikipedia.org/?oldid=371542698 *Contributors*:

Internal arcuate fibers *Source*: http://en.wikipedia.org/?oldid=389481321 *Contributors*: Malcolma

Dorsal column nuclei *Source*: http://en.wikipedia.org/?oldid=332262592 *Contributors*:

Prethalamus *Source*: http://en.wikipedia.org/?oldid=335414697 *Contributors*: JaysonSunshine

Pyramid (brainstem) *Source*: http://en.wikipedia.org/?oldid=386279842 *Contributors*: Xezbeth

Cerebral crus *Source*: http://en.wikipedia.org/?oldid=352959140 *Contributors*: Eleassar

Anterolateral sulcus of medulla *Source*: http://en.wikipedia.org/?oldid=377268308 *Contributors*: Malcolma

Thalamic fasciculus *Source*: http://en.wikipedia.org/?oldid=327763843 *Contributors*: Arcadian

Lenticular fasciculus *Source*: http://en.wikipedia.org/?oldid=327768490 *Contributors*: Arcadian

Anterior cochlear nucleus *Source*: http://en.wikipedia.org/?oldid=359155699 *Contributors*: Goodvac

Pallidothalamic tracts *Source*: http://en.wikipedia.org/?oldid=329982262 *Contributors*: Arcadian

Pontine micturition center *Source*: http://en.wikipedia.org/?oldid=390015895 *Contributors*: Wisdom89

Fields of forel *Source*: http://en.wikipedia.org/?oldid=358152202 *Contributors*: Rberlow

Image Sources, Licenses and Contributors

file:Illu pituitary pineal glands.jpg *Source*: http://en.wikipedia.org/w/index.php?title=File:Illu_pituitary_pineal_glands.jpg *License*: Public Domain *Contributors*: Denniss, Lennert B, Patho, Was a bee, 2 anonymous edits

file:Gray694.png *Source*: http://en.wikipedia.org/w/index.php?title=File:Gray694.png *License*: unknown *Contributors*: Arcadian, Lipothymia, Skies

Image:Illu cerebrum lobes.jpg *Source*: http://en.wikipedia.org/w/index.php?title=File:Illu_cerebrum_lobes.jpg *License*: Public Domain *Contributors*: Arcadian, Was a bee

Image:Gray677.png *Source*: http://en.wikipedia.org/w/index.php?title=File:Gray677.png *License*: unknown *Contributors*: Arcadian, Was a bee, 1 anonymous edits

Image:Gray679.png *Source*: http://en.wikipedia.org/w/index.php?title=File:Gray679.png *License*: unknown *Contributors*: Brim, Dodo, Lipothymia, Was a bee

Image:Gray687.png *Source*: http://en.wikipedia.org/w/index.php?title=File:Gray687.png *License*: Public Domain *Contributors*: Arcadian, Lipothymia

Image:Gray688.png *Source*: http://en.wikipedia.org/w/index.php?title=File:Gray688.png *License*: unknown *Contributors*: Arcadian, Lipothymia

Image:Gray695.png *Source*: http://en.wikipedia.org/w/index.php?title=File:Gray695.png *License*: unknown *Contributors*: Arcadian, Lipothymia

Image:Gray700.png *Source*: http://en.wikipedia.org/w/index.php?title=File:Gray700.png *License*: Public Domain *Contributors*: Arcadian, Lipothymia, 1 anonymous edits

Image:Gray714.png *Source*: http://en.wikipedia.org/w/index.php?title=File:Gray714.png *License*: unknown *Contributors*: Arcadian, Lipothymia

Image:Gray715.png *Source*: http://en.wikipedia.org/w/index.php?title=File:Gray715.png *License*: unknown *Contributors*: Arcadian, Aude, Lipothymia, Origamiemensch, Quibik, Was a bee, 1 anonymous edits

Image:Gray724.png *Source*: http://en.wikipedia.org/w/index.php?title=File:Gray724.png *License*: unknown *Contributors*: Arcadian, Archfalhwyl, Lipothymia, Was a bee, 2 anonymous edits

Image:Gray768.png *Source*: http://en.wikipedia.org/w/index.php?title=File:Gray768.png *License*: unknown *Contributors*: Arcadian, Was a bee, 1 anonymous edits

Image:Human cerebrum lateral view, a part of temporal lobe resected description.JPG *Source*: http://en.wikipedia.org/w/index.php?title=File:Human_cerebrum_lateral_view,_a_part_of_temporal_lobe_resected_description.JPG *License*: Creative Commons Attribution 2.5 *Contributors*: John A Beal, PhD Dep't. of Cellular Biology & Anatomy, Louisiana State University Health Sciences Center Shreveport

Image:Human brain frontal (coronal) section description.JPG *Source*: http://en.wikipedia.org/w/index.php?title=File:Human_brain_frontal_(coronal)_section_description.JPG *License*: Creative Commons Attribution 2.5 *Contributors*: John A Beal, PhD Dep't. of Cellular Biology & Anatomy, Louisiana State University Health Sciences Center Shreveport

file:Gray768.png *Source*: http://en.wikipedia.org/w/index.php?title=File:Gray768.png *License*: unknown *Contributors*: Arcadian, Was a bee, 1 anonymous edits

file:Gray679.png *Source*: http://en.wikipedia.org/w/index.php?title=File:Gray679.png *License*: unknown *Contributors*: Brim, Dodo, Lipothymia, Was a bee

Image:Gray682.png *Source*: http://en.wikipedia.org/w/index.php?title=File:Gray682.png *License*: Public Domain *Contributors*: Arcadian, OldakQuill

Image:Gray689.png *Source*: http://en.wikipedia.org/w/index.php?title=File:Gray689.png *License*: unknown *Contributors*: Arcadian, Lipothymia

Image:Gray701.png *Source*: http://en.wikipedia.org/w/index.php?title=File:Gray701.png *License*: unknown *Contributors*: Arcadian, Delldot, Fidech, Skies, Was a bee, 1 anonymous edits

Image:Gray705.png *Source*: http://en.wikipedia.org/w/index.php?title=File:Gray705.png *License*: unknown *Contributors*: Arcadian, Lipothymia, Was a bee

Image:Gray707.png *Source*: http://en.wikipedia.org/w/index.php?title=File:Gray707.png *License*: unknown *Contributors*: Arcadian, Lipothymia, Quibik, Was a bee

Image:Gray708.svg *Source*: http://en.wikipedia.org/w/index.php?title=File:Gray708.svg *License*: unknown *Contributors*: lyhana8

Image:Gray717.png *Source*: http://en.wikipedia.org/w/index.php?title=File:Gray717.png *License*: unknown *Contributors*: Arcadian, Lipothymia, Was a bee

Image:Gray719.png *Source*: http://en.wikipedia.org/w/index.php?title=File:Gray719.png *License*: unknown *Contributors*: Arcadian, Lipothymia, Mormegil, Was a bee

Image:Gray720.png *Source*: http://en.wikipedia.org/w/index.php?title=File:Gray720.png *License*: unknown *Contributors*: Arcadian, Lipothymia, Was a bee

Image:Gray745.png *Source*: http://en.wikipedia.org/w/index.php?title=File:Gray745.png *License*: unknown *Contributors*: Arcadian, Lipothymia, Magnus Manske, Was a bee

Image:Gray760.png *Source*: http://en.wikipedia.org/w/index.php?title=File:Gray760.png *License*: unknown *Contributors*: Arcadian, Lipothymia, 1 anonymous edits

Image:Gray761.png *Source*: http://en.wikipedia.org/w/index.php?title=File:Gray761.png *License*: unknown *Contributors*: Arcadian, Lipothymia

Image:Gray1180.png *Source*: http://en.wikipedia.org/w/index.php?title=File:Gray1180.png *License*: Public Domain *Contributors*: Arcadian, Lipothymia, Was a bee, 1 anonymous edits

Image:Illu pituitary pineal glands.jpg *Source*: http://en.wikipedia.org/w/index.php?title=File:Illu_pituitary_pineal_glands.jpg *License*: Public Domain *Contributors*: Denniss, Lennert B, Patho, Was a bee, 2 anonymous edits

Image:Human brainstem anterior view 2 description.JPG *Source*: http://en.wikipedia.org/w/index.php?title=File:Human_brainstem_anterior_view_2_description.JPG *License*: Creative Commons Attribution 2.5 *Contributors*: John A Beal, PhD Dep't. of Cellular Biology & Anatomy, Louisiana State University Health Sciences Center Shreveport

file:Gray719.png *Source*: http://en.wikipedia.org/w/index.php?title=File:Gray719.png *License*: unknown *Contributors*: Arcadian, Lipothymia, Mormegil, Was a bee

Image:Human_brain_frontal_(coronal)_section_description.JPG *Source*: http://en.wikipedia.org/w/index.php?title=File:Human_brain_frontal_(coronal)_section_description.JPG *License*: Creative Commons Attribution 2.5 *Contributors*: John A Beal, PhD Dep't. of Cellular Biology & Anatomy, Louisiana State University Health Sciences Center Shreveport

Image:Brainlobes.svg *Source*: http://en.wikipedia.org/w/index.php?title=File:Brainlobes.svg *License*: unknown *Contributors*: User:King of Hearts

file:Human brain inferior view description.JPG *Source*: http://en.wikipedia.org/w/index.php?title=File:Human_brain_inferior_view_description.JPG *License*: Creative Commons Attribution 2.5 *Contributors*: John A Beal, PhD Dep't. of Cellular Biology & Anatomy, Louisiana State University Health Sciences Center Shreveport

file:Human brainstem-thalamus posterior view description.JPG *Source*: http://en.wikipedia.org/w/index.php?title=File:Human_brainstem-thalamus_posterior_view_description.JPG *License*: Creative Commons Attribution 2.5 *Contributors*: John A Beal, PhD Dep't. of Cellular Biology & Anatomy, Louisiana State University Health Sciences Center Shreveport

Image:Midbrainsuperiorcolliculus.png *Source*: http://en.wikipedia.org/w/index.php?title=File:Midbrainsuperiorcolliculus.png *License*: GNU Free Documentation License *Contributors*: AxelBoldt, Lipothymia

Image:Ventral midbrain.png *Source*: http://en.wikipedia.org/w/index.php?title=File:Ventral_midbrain.png *License*: Creative Commons Attribution 2.5 *Contributors*: P. Read Montague

Image:midbrainsuperiorcolliculus.png *Source*: http://en.wikipedia.org/w/index.php?title=File:Midbrainsuperiorcolliculus.png *License*: GNU Free Documentation License *Contributors*: AxelBoldt, Lipothymia

Image:Gray18.png *Source*: http://en.wikipedia.org/w/index.php?title=File:Gray18.png *License*: unknown *Contributors*: User Magnus Manske on en.wikipedia

Image:Gray40.png *Source*: http://en.wikipedia.org/w/index.php?title=File:Gray40.png *License*: unknown *Contributors*: User Magnus Manske on en.wikipedia

Image:Gray711.png *Source*: http://en.wikipedia.org/w/index.php?title=File:Gray711.png *License*: unknown *Contributors*: Arcadian, Lipothymia, OldakQuill

Image:Gray712.png *Source*: http://en.wikipedia.org/w/index.php?title=File:Gray712.png *License*: unknown *Contributors*: Arcadian, Lipothymia

Image:EmbryonicBrain.svg *Source*: http://en.wikipedia.org/w/index.php?title=File:EmbryonicBrain.svg *License*: Creative Commons Attribution-Sharealike 2.5 *Contributors*: User:Nrets, User:Surachit

Image:internal view of basal ganglia.jpg *Source*: http://en.wikipedia.org/w/index.php?title=File:Internal_view_of_basal_ganglia.jpg *License*: Public Domain *Contributors*: User:Paul Verheggen

Image:external view of basal ganglia.jpg *Source*: http://en.wikipedia.org/w/index.php?title=File:External_view_of_basal_ganglia.jpg *License*: Public Domain *Contributors*: User:Paul Verheggen

Image:anterior face of brainstem.jpg *Source*: http://en.wikipedia.org/w/index.php?title=File:Anterior_face_of_brainstem.jpg *License*: Public Domain *Contributors*: User:Paul Verheggen

Image:posterior face of brainstem.jpg *Source*: http://en.wikipedia.org/w/index.php?title=File:Posterior_face_of_brainstem.jpg *License*: Public Domain *Contributors*: User:Paul Verheggen

Image:external face of brainstem.jpg *Source*: http://en.wikipedia.org/w/index.php?title=File:External_face_of_brainstem.jpg *License*: Public Domain *Contributors*: User:Paul Verheggen

file:Gray759.png *Source*: http://en.wikipedia.org/w/index.php?title=File:Gray759.png *License*: unknown *Contributors*: Arcadian, Lipothymia, Was a bee

file:Gray710.png *Source*: http://en.wikipedia.org/w/index.php?title=File:Gray710.png *License*: Public Domain *Contributors*: Arcadian, Lipothymia, Was a bee, 2 anonymous edits

Image:Gray685.png *Source*: http://en.wikipedia.org/w/index.php?title=File:Gray685.png *License*: Public Domain *Contributors*: Arcadian, Lipothymia

Image:Gray690.png *Source*: http://en.wikipedia.org/w/index.php?title=File:Gray690.png *License*: unknown *Contributors*: Arcadian, Lipothymia

Image:Gray713.png *Source*: http://en.wikipedia.org/w/index.php?title=File:Gray713.png *License*: unknown *Contributors*: Arcadian, Lipothymia, Was a bee

file:Gray695.png *Source*: http://en.wikipedia.org/w/index.php?title=File:Gray695.png *License*: unknown *Contributors*: Arcadian, Lipothymia

Image:Gray694.png *Source*: http://en.wikipedia.org/w/index.php?title=File:Gray694.png *License*: unknown *Contributors*: Arcadian, Lipothymia, Skies

Image:Gray696.png *Source*: http://en.wikipedia.org/w/index.php?title=File:Gray696.png *License*: Public Domain *Contributors*: Arcadian, Lipothymia, Mcstrother

Image:Gray697.png *Source*: http://en.wikipedia.org/w/index.php?title=File:Gray697.png *License*: unknown *Contributors*: Arcadian, Lipothymia

file:Gray711.png *Source*: http://en.wikipedia.org/w/index.php?title=File:Gray711.png *License*: unknown *Contributors*: Arcadian, Lipothymia, OldakQuill

Image:Gray680.png *Source*: http://en.wikipedia.org/w/index.php?title=File:Gray680.png *License*: Public Domain *Contributors*: Arcadian

Image:ThreeNeuronArc.png *Source*: http://en.wikipedia.org/w/index.php?title=File:ThreeNeuronArc.png *License*: GNU Free Documentation License *Contributors*: Original uploader was Tvil at en.wikipedia

file:Lateral_lemniscus.PNG *Source*: http://en.wikipedia.org/w/index.php?title=File:Lateral_lemniscus.PNG *License*: unknown *Contributors*: User:Mikael Häggström

Image:Gray683.png *Source*: http://en.wikipedia.org/w/index.php?title=File:Gray683.png *License*: Public Domain *Contributors*: Arcadian

Image:Gray684.png *Source*: http://en.wikipedia.org/w/index.php?title=File:Gray684.png *License*: unknown *Contributors*: Arcadian, Lipothymia

Image:Gray691.png *Source*: http://en.wikipedia.org/w/index.php?title=File:Gray691.png *License*: unknown *Contributors*: Arcadian, Lipothymia

Image:Gray710.png *Source*: http://en.wikipedia.org/w/index.php?title=File:Gray710.png *License*: Public Domain *Contributors*: Arcadian, Lipothymia, Was a bee, 2 anonymous edits

file:Gray709.png *Source*: http://en.wikipedia.org/w/index.php?title=File:Gray709.png *License*: unknown *Contributors*: Arcadian, Lipothymia

file:Gray734.png *Source*: http://en.wikipedia.org/w/index.php?title=File:Gray734.png *License*: unknown *Contributors*: Arcadian, Lipothymia, Materialscientist, Mormegil, Quibik

file:Gray735.png *Source*: http://en.wikipedia.org/w/index.php?title=File:Gray735.png *License*: unknown *Contributors*: Arcadian, Lipothymia, Mormegil

Image:Gray699.png *Source*: http://en.wikipedia.org/w/index.php?title=File:Gray699.png *License*: unknown *Contributors*: Arcadian, Lipothymia, Skies

Image:Gray704.png *Source*: http://en.wikipedia.org/w/index.php?title=File:Gray704.png *License*: unknown *Contributors*: Arcadian, Lipothymia

Image:Gray709.png *Source*: http://en.wikipedia.org/w/index.php?title=File:Gray709.png *License*: unknown *Contributors*: Arcadian, Lipothymia

Image:Gray736.png *Source*: http://en.wikipedia.org/w/index.php?title=File:Gray736.png *License*: unknown *Contributors*: Arcadian, Mormegil, 2 anonymous edits

file:Gray691.png *Source*: http://en.wikipedia.org/w/index.php?title=File:Gray691.png *License*: unknown *Contributors*: Arcadian, Lipothymia

Image:Gray692.png *Source*: http://en.wikipedia.org/w/index.php?title=File:Gray692.png *License*: Public Domain *Contributors*: Arcadian, Lipothymia

Image:Gray753.png *Source*: http://en.wikipedia.org/w/index.php?title=File:Gray753.png *License*: unknown *Contributors*: Arcadian, Lipothymia, Magnus Manske, Was a bee

Image:Gray759.png *Source*: http://en.wikipedia.org/w/index.php?title=File:Gray759.png *License*: unknown *Contributors*: Arcadian, Lipothymia, Was a bee

file:cn3nucleus.png *Source*: http://en.wikipedia.org/w/index.php?title=File:Cn3nucleus.png *License*: GNU Free Documentation License *Contributors*: AxelBoldt, Lipothymia, Maquesta, Una Smith, 2 anonymous edits

file:Gray722.png *Source*: http://en.wikipedia.org/w/index.php?title=File:Gray722.png *License*: unknown *Contributors*: Arcadian, Lipothymia, Was a bee

Image:Cod brain showing tectum.png *Source*: http://en.wikipedia.org/w/index.php?title=File:Cod_brain_showing_tectum.png *License*: Public Domain *Contributors*: user:Looie496

Image:SparrowTectum.jpg *Source*: http://en.wikipedia.org/w/index.php?title=File:SparrowTectum.jpg *License*: Public Domain *Contributors*: Chrislb, Daniel 1992, Feezil, Innotata, 1 anonymous edits

File:HE stain murine optic tectum.jpg *Source*: http://en.wikipedia.org/w/index.php?title=File:HE_stain_murine_optic_tectum.jpg *License*: Creative Commons Attribution-Sharealike 2.0 *Contributors*: User:CopperKettle

Image:Isthmii circuit.svg *Source*: http://en.wikipedia.org/w/index.php?title=File:Isthmii_circuit.svg *License*: GNU Free Documentation License *Contributors*: User:Looie496

file:Gray685.png *Source*: http://en.wikipedia.org/w/index.php?title=File:Gray685.png *License*: Public Domain *Contributors*: Arcadian, Lipothymia

Image:Gray678.png *Source*: http://en.wikipedia.org/w/index.php?title=File:Gray678.png *License*: unknown *Contributors*: Arcadian, Filip em, Lipothymia, Was a bee

Image:Gehirn, basal - beschriftet lat.svg *Source*: http://en.wikipedia.org/w/index.php?title=File:Gehirn,_basal_-_beschriftet_lat.svg *License*: Creative Commons Attribution-Sharealike 2.5 *Contributors*: User:NEUROtiker

file:Constudthal.gif *Source*: http://en.wikipedia.org/w/index.php?title=File:Constudthal.gif *License*: GNU Free Documentation License *Contributors*: Original uploader was RobinH at en.wikibooks

file:Gray696.png *Source*: http://en.wikipedia.org/w/index.php?title=File:Gray696.png *License*: Public Domain *Contributors*: Arcadian, Lipothymia, Mcstrother

Image:Gray774.png *Source*: http://en.wikipedia.org/w/index.php?title=File:Gray774.png *License*: unknown *Contributors*: Arcadian, Lipothymia, Magnus Manske, Was a bee, רואיל

Image:Gray785.png *Source*: http://en.wikipedia.org/w/index.php?title=File:Gray785.png *License*: unknown *Contributors*: Arcadian, Kersti Nebelsiek, Lipothymia, Magnus Manske

Image:Brain stem sagittal section.svg *Source*: http://en.wikipedia.org/w/index.php?title=File:Brain_stem_sagittal_section.svg *License*: Attribution *Contributors*: Patrick J. Lynch, medical illustrator

file:EmbryonicBrain.svg *Source*: http://en.wikipedia.org/w/index.php?title=File:EmbryonicBrain.svg *License*: Creative Commons Attribution-Sharealike 2.5 *Contributors*: User:Nrets, User:Surachit

file:Gray708.svg *Source*: http://en.wikipedia.org/w/index.php?title=File:Gray708.svg *License*: unknown *Contributors*: lyhana8

File:CerebCircuit.png *Source*: http://en.wikipedia.org/w/index.php?title=File:CerebCircuit.png *License*: unknown *Contributors*: Was a bee

file:Gray707.png *Source*: http://en.wikipedia.org/w/index.php?title=File:Gray707.png *License*: unknown *Contributors*: Arcadian, Lipothymia, Quibik, Was a bee

Image:Gray716.png *Source*: http://en.wikipedia.org/w/index.php?title=File:Gray716.png *License*: unknown *Contributors*: Arcadian, Lipothymia, Was a bee

Image:Gray792.png *Source*: http://en.wikipedia.org/w/index.php?title=File:Gray792.png *License*: unknown *Contributors*: Arcadian, Magnus Manske

file:Gray649.png *Source*: http://en.wikipedia.org/w/index.php?title=File:Gray649.png *License*: Public Domain *Contributors*: Arcadian, Erfil, Was a bee

file:Gray788.png *Source*: http://en.wikipedia.org/w/index.php?title=File:Gray788.png *License*: unknown *Contributors*: Arcadian, Lipothymia, Magnus Manske

file:Gray760.png *Source*: http://en.wikipedia.org/w/index.php?title=File:Gray760.png *License*: unknown *Contributors*: Arcadian, Lipothymia, 1 anonymous edits

Image:Gray698.png *Source*: http://en.wikipedia.org/w/index.php?title=File:Gray698.png *License*: unknown *Contributors*: Arcadian, Lipothymia

file:Human caudal brainstem posterior view description.JPG *Source*: http://en.wikipedia.org/w/index.php?title=File:Human_caudal_brainstem_posterior_view_description.JPG *License*: Creative Commons Attribution 2.5 *Contributors*: John A Beal, PhD Dep't. of Cellular Biology & Anatomy, Louisiana State University Health Sciences Center Shreveport

Image:Gray693.png *Source*: http://en.wikipedia.org/w/index.php?title=File:Gray693.png *License*: unknown *Contributors*: Arcadian, Lipothymia

file:Cn3nucleus.png *Source*: http://en.wikipedia.org/w/index.php?title=File:Cn3nucleus.png *License*: GNU Free Documentation License *Contributors*: AxelBoldt, Lipothymia, Maquesta, Una Smith, 2 anonymous edits

Image:Human brain frontal (coronal) section description 2.JPG *Source*: http://en.wikipedia.org/w/index.php?title=File:Human_brain_frontal_(coronal)_section_description_2.JPG *License*: Creative Commons Attribution 2.5 *Contributors*: John A Beal, PhD Dep't. of Cellular Biology & Anatomy, Louisiana State University Health Sciences Center Shreveport

file:Gray700.png *Source*: http://en.wikipedia.org/w/index.php?title=File:Gray700.png *License*: Public Domain *Contributors*: Arcadian, Lipothymia, 1 anonymous edits

file:DA-loops in PD.jpg *Source*: http://en.wikipedia.org/w/index.php?title=File:DA-loops_in_PD.jpg *License*: Creative Commons Attribution 2.5 *Contributors*: Chris 73, Malyszkz, Najibeltecle, Penubag, Xhienne, 1 anonymous edits

CPSIA information can be obtained at www.ICGtesting.com
Printed in the USA
LVOW111930080113

314840LV00005B/137/P